A MAN'S WAY THROUGH

THE TWELVE STEPS

A MAN'S WAY THROUGH

THE TWELVE STEPS

by Dan Griffin, M.A.

HAZELDEN®

Hazelden
Center City, Minnesota 55012
hazelden.org

Library of Congress Cataloging-in-Publication Data

Griffin, Dan, 1972–
    A man's way through the twelve steps / Dan Griffin.
        p.   cm.
    Includes bibliographical references.
    ISBN 978-1-59285-724-1 (softcover)
    1. Twelve-step programs. 2. Alcoholics—Rehabilitation. 3. Men—
Psychology. 4. Masculinity. 5. Emotions. I. Title.
    HV5278.G75 2009
    616.86'106—dc22

                                            2009027612

Editor's note
The names, details, and circumstances may have been changed to protect the privacy of those mentioned in this publication.

This publication is not intended as a substitute for the advice of health care professionals.

16 15 14   5 6 7

Cover design by David Spohn
Interior design by David Swanson
Typesetting by BookMobile Design and Publishing Services

This book is dedicated to
the memory of my father,
Dr. Owen Martin Griffin,
who never got the gift of recovery;
the men upon whose shoulders I stand;
those who walk the path with me today;
and those yet to find their way.

The Guy in the Glass
by
Dale Wimbrow (1895–1954)

When you get what you want in your struggle for pelf,*
And the world makes you King for a day,
Then go to the mirror and look at yourself,
And see what that guy has to say.

For it isn't your Father, or Mother, or Wife,
Whose judgement upon you must pass.
The feller whose verdict counts most in your life
Is the guy staring back from the glass.

He's the feller to please, never mind all the rest,
For he's with you clear up to the end,
And you've passed your most dangerous, difficult test
If the guy in the glass is your friend.

You may be like Jack Horner and "chisel" a plum,
And think you're a wonderful guy,
But the man in the glass says you're only a bum
If you can't look him straight in the eye.

You can fool the whole world down the pathway of years,
And get pats on the back as you pass,
But your final reward will be heartaches and tears
If you've cheated the guy in the glass.

* pelf — riches, gold

Contents

In 1995, at the age of twenty-three, I was just over a year sober and my father had just died from complications due to chronic alcoholism. At the wake, some men from one of my father's AA meetings invited me to attend a recovery retreat, even paying for my airfare and registration.

The disappointment started as soon as the men picked me up. One of the men immediately started complaining about his wife and then told a derogatory joke about women. Laughter filled the car like smoke and I laughed, too, though hesitantly. The conversation went on to span relationships, sports, recovery—from the mundane to profane to the inane. As we arrived at the retreat center, I could see water from a small lake in the distance with tall trees quietly swaying back and forth, welcoming us and promising solitude. Shortly after we arrived one of the men told an offensive and racist joke. This time I did not laugh. Walking away down toward the water, I thought to myself, "Is this the best we can do as men? Is this what I have to look forward to in my relationships with men in recovery?" That day I made a commitment to myself that I would not cheapen my recovery by compromising my values just so that I could fit in. Easier said than done.

The path to who we can become is rocky and full of mistakes, but recovery offers us the opportunity to learn from those mistakes, to grow, and to change how we live. When we need guidance on our path, we learn to look to others in recovery for help. Those who actively work the Twelve Steps know that when we challenge each other according to the principles of the program, we support each other in becoming the best that we can be.

As a man reading this book, you will ask questions about who you have been, who you are, and who you will become in recovery—and you will find that the answers are embodied in the principles of the Twelve Steps. You will see that some of what you have been told, learned, and even thought about men has been inaccurate. You will also see that there is no resource greater than the Steps to help affirm what is best about our masculinity and about being men. What we are experiencing in the Twelve Step culture is much bigger than the very personal transformation that we experience and witness in others. Every time we take a risk and share honestly from our hearts, we create an opportunity for others to do the same and transform how men live as men—one man at a time.

⚱

ACKNOWLEDGMENTS

This book started as an idea many years ago. To every man and woman who has supported me and the idea; to all of those with whom I have sat in the circles of recovery: thank you.

Joe Moriarity, who patiently and painstakingly guided me through the painful process of cutting the rock away. Sid Farrar, thank you for your unwavering support and steady steering of the ship. Thank you to all of the staff of Hazelden Publishing who helped in the completion of this book.

Great thanks to the Review Crew: Priscilla, Ben, Larry, Bob, and Eric. Special thanks to Dave Farley who went above and beyond to offer feedback and read draft after draft.

Special thanks to Peter Bell for his guidance and feedback on "Responding to Difference."

Dr. Larry Anderson provided invaluable feedback on some of the toughest parts of this book including "Men, Violence, and Trauma." Jim Nelson, you gently guided me on the path so many years ago. Earl Hipp, you helped a rookie get through this.

Thank you to Christine Reil for painstakingly transcribing all interviews.

To Mike Driscoll, Barb Hughes, Jon Harper, and Cathy

Huberty: you lit the lantern, carried the lantern, and then gave me the lantern and because of that I am no longer in the dark.

The Band of Seven Brothers: you carried me through this. Thank you.

Bill, you are the father I never had; Ben, you are the older brother I never had; and Eric, you are the sponsor I needed because you led me to myself.

Finally, they say that behind every successful man is a great woman. I am truly blessed to have three: My mom, Sherry, who never gave up on me; Dr. Stephanie Covington, I honor you for your courage in blazing the trail and your generosity in inviting me to walk with you—this book would not exist without you—thank you for believing in me; Nancy, my partner and soul mate, you are my love, my life. Thank you for loving me for who I am and teaching me how to do the same. My love always, LB.

SPECIAL ACKNOWLEDGMENTS

To the men who, without hesitation, made themselves available for interviews, follow-up questions, and last-minute requests: Brian B., Rob S., Juan H., Dan J., West H., Rich V., Kit S., Joe P., Joe H., Gary R., Kerry D., Mike H., Reggie B., Brandon F., Dave F., Charlie B., Andy M., Chris A., Quinn D., Jo C., Steve S., Peter K., Paul S., Vang B., Casey K., Mike M., Mike J., Dominique M., Larry A., and Miguel B.

Each man put a part of his heart and soul in my hands, and I thank you for that. I hope that I have honored your life experience. Your collective experience, strength, and hope gave this book life. Thank you.

In memory of Ryane Frank, a young man who changed my life forever.

For all of the young boys in this world, that you may find peace and the courage, support, and love to be yourselves. Let nobody stand in your way.

INTRODUCTION

Regardless of your background and previous experiences, when you come into treatment or a Twelve Step program, you immediately experience a culture in which people communicate. You too are asked, even expected, to communicate in ways with which you as a man are probably neither familiar nor comfortable. Thus begins the most exciting and rewarding journey you will ever take on this earth: a man's journey through the Twelve Steps.

This book is written to all men in Twelve Step recovery. The "we" and the "you" I speak to in this book are all of us men charting the courses of our lives by the shining light of the Twelve Steps.

Many of us have never thought about what being a man has to do with our recovery. Unlike our female counterparts, we have not spent the last twenty years looking at what we need, taking care of ourselves, and learning to live full lives. Even the Twelve Step community has been reluctant to discuss the freedom of expression for men inherent in the philosophy of the Twelve Steps. Many still assume that "men are the way they are," and they don't see the pain, struggles, and limitations of men suffocating in the "box of masculinity" as it's been defined by our society.

So it is that *A Man's Way through the Twelve Steps* has

some history in the Women's Movement, a time when women began to look at their lives and the effect society's "rules" had on how they were raised. Because of that important and historical work, women today have a deeper and clearer sense of what it means to be female and how social messages have limited and restricted them. The concept of gender and the socially created roles for males and females have evolved. The rules and expectations for men have changed. Today it's easier to recognize how the ways we are raised create limitations for *both* men and women.

A Man's Way also has its history in the Men's Movement. When women began looking at their lives through the lens of gender, some courageous men concluded that we needed to do the same. Far less work has been done on the impact of gender on men's lives, particularly in relation to addiction and recovery. This book helps to fill that void. *A Man's Way* is about creating gender awareness for men in recovery. It will help you look more closely at the realities of your life, and address and respond to the challenges we face as men in Western society.

Who am I? When you ask that question at the beginning of your recovery journey, you are probably able to say with total honesty: "I don't know."

What does it mean to be a man? As a man, you may accept certain ways of thinking, talking, and acting as just who you are. You probably don't see that our culture has a set of rules for being a man. You may not realize you are following a kind of script. You put on your costume and act out the script. Your addictions to drugs, gambling, sex, rage, or relationships are part of the fabric of your costume that allows you to hide your true self.

This book is meant in part to be a wake-up call. My hope is that, as a result of reading this book, you will think about your ideas of what it means to be a man and about your life as a man in recovery. *A Man's Way* will not address all of the challenges and issues men face today, but it will help you confront the changes you need to make in your life. You will find parts of yourself that you had long forgotten, had tried to get away from, and that you never knew existed.

Throughout the book I will look at how men are raised— some of these discussions will apply to you and some will not. However, my hope is that you will begin to form better ideas of who you are as a man. How you see yourself as a man affects how you see the Steps, how you engage in your recovery, and what you see as problems. These perceptions also can limit how much you grow in your recovery, especially in your relationships with other men and women.

A Man's Way has the book *A Woman's Way through the Twelve Steps* as a core part of its foundation. In this groundbreaking book, Dr. Stephanie Covington looked at the Twelve Steps and their impact on women's lives. She was able to stay true to the principles in the Twelve Steps while broadening the canvass upon which women paint their recovery. I have attempted to do the same for men by borrowing her model of using interviews and discussions of each Step to help you better understand how each Step relates to your life and to the lives of men in general.

As men in recovery, we have addiction and the destruction it has caused in common. We also share a common solution: the Twelve Steps. With every step we take toward loving ourselves and shedding parts of our costume, we begin to see the limitless possibilities for who we can be and how we can live our lives. With that vision comes the freedom to be who we are, regardless of society's box of masculinity. By being true to ourselves, we automatically become the best men we can be.

I begin this book by looking at what is often one of the most difficult issues men have to deal with in sobriety: recognizing and expressing our feelings. How we come to terms with our emotions has a big impact on how effectively we are able to work a Twelve Step program. I then explore each Step with a focus on the unique cultural, social, and personal challenges and perspectives that men bring to understanding and applying that Step in their lives. Finally, I cover four topics—grief, relationships, violence and trauma, and difference—that deserve their own chapters because of their complexity and how vital they are for men in achieving quality, long-term sobriety.

Throughout the book you will discover stories from others who have been on this journey for some time. Draw on their insights and experiences to find the strength and hope to carry you through difficult moments. Explore the many questions raised in the discussions, and envision the limitless options available to us as men. I hope that as you read this book, you will look deeply at who you are and the life you want to live.

Take what you want and leave the rest. As my first sponsor always told me, misery is optional.

FEELINGS

*I came into recovery with the mind-set
that you have to deny all feelings;
feelings were the enemy.*

– PETER –

Shortly after my father's funeral, I was helping my mom clean the house when I found some notes my father had written while in treatment. As I looked through them, I realized that he didn't think anybody could help him, felt alone a lot of the time, and didn't think he could talk to anyone. I had not known that he had those struggles or that he felt lonely, insecure, or fearful. He always acted as though everything was under control and that he didn't need anything from anyone. He always seemed quite self-assured. Something led my father to believe that the only way he could survive those feelings was to drink them away. He was not going to open up about them, even if shutting down killed him. And it did. Tragically, far too many men are walking the same path. Don't talk, don't trust, and don't feel—it's the unwritten code by which many men live their lives.

The most compelling responses I received from the men I interviewed focused on how recovery has given them awareness of the many feelings they actually had and the ability to accept, appreciate, and, most important, communicate the degree to which, as men, they experience the range of human emotion. If men who are not addicts ignore their feelings, they miss the fullness of life and close the door on an essential part of who they are. We addicts ignore our feelings at our own peril. Being aware of how we feel is a matter of life or death for us. Our feelings are both essential parts of who we are as men and the foundation of our recovery, and this chapter explores how we are raised to accept and reject our feelings.

Burying the Caveman

If feelings are a core part of the human experience, then they must be a core part of our recovery, too. I have yet to meet a man who does not feel the whole range of emotions. I have yet to meet a man who grew up knowing how to express what he was feeling, when he was feeling it, without allowing those feelings to mean anything about his masculinity. Andy, a fifty-eight-year-old IT consultant with twenty-six years in Al-Anon, talked about this:

> *All men have feelings, whether or not they want to admit it. I came into the program not knowing how to name what I was feeling. Now, after years of practice, I can name them and experience and acknowledge all the feelings that I have, whether or not they are manly.*

Joe H., a forty-two-year-old with five years of sobriety who owns his own insurance agency, talked about the paradox regarding men and our experience of emotion:

I am emotionally complex like I believed only women were. I've found that I saw them this way because they were the only gender I saw expressing themselves emotionally.

So long as we perpetuate the lie that men do not have feelings, we will believe this to be true because, as Joe H. said, we will only see women expressing their feelings. Whether or not we are aware of our feelings, we do have them.

Dave, a forty-two-year-old stay-at-home dad with twenty-one years of long-term recovery, described his experience:

In my youth, emotions ruled my decisions. I couldn't necessarily articulate my feelings surrounding specific decisions, but their rule over me was undeniable.

Few of us come into recovery knowing how to open up and share what is happening in our lives. It's our task as men to learn how to integrate our feelings into our lives in a meaningful and helpful way. Joe H. verbalizes what many men experience as they come into recovery:

Prior to recovery I did not have practice in expressing how I felt. Nor did I know how to recognize how I felt. Usually when I did express myself, it was using anger as a result of all the other emotions not being expressed.

One of the many lies we tell about ourselves on a daily basis is connected with how we feel. We learn to deny many of our feelings, and in doing so we lie to ourselves. We learn to lie from the people closest to us. Then, we become alienated from our feelings, and that alienation seeps into our relationships and defines them. Joe H. added a little humor to his idea of feelings before he got into recovery:

If you talk about feelings, you can't be macho. It goes back to the caveman days: go kill your meal, bring it back, and throw it at your woman and you're done. You didn't have to talk about your feelings.

Today, as a father of two young girls, Joe H. will be the first person to tell you that trying to live this way was killing him and his relationships. Even after five years sober, he knows he's still learning how to express what he's really feeling.

From Day One

As soon as we are born it starts. Baby boys, identified by their cute little blue blanket, are held less. Soothed less. Handled a little more roughly. Pay attention, and you'll see six-year-old boys who are well on their way to learning the rules of masculinity. That's heartbreaking. Juan, a forty-three-year-old sales and marketing consultant with eighteen years of long-term recovery, remembers vividly how he responded to his parents' divorce as a young boy:

My parents divorced when I was very young, and I remember very clearly a conversation that I had with God and saying, "I will never let anybody fucking hurt me again." I remember [creating] a wall . . . I was eight years old at the time . . . And I remember that tape playing as the years went on. I remember a girlfriend calling me "The Ice Man" because I would shut down my emotions. That plagued me for years.

Young boys everywhere are having experiences like this! The young boy left to comfort himself as his parent coldly walks away from him, telling him to "be a big boy." The boy who learns that being tough means using force to get what he wants. The young man who thinks he shouldn't hug Dad anymore, and as a result comes to see his body only as a sexual object. These are just some of the messages we hear as we grow up. Rejecting how we feel and teasing or shaming others for how they feel become part of who we are without our realizing it.

Nothing More than Feelings

Most of us are taught from a very young age to focus on our thoughts and ignore our feelings. As men in recovery, this is something we cannot afford to do if we value our sobriety. "At the beginning of my recovery, I learned from my sponsor that addiction is a feelings disease," said Joe P., who has twenty years of long-term recovery and is the executive director of a treatment center for individuals with co-occurring disorders.

As soon as we begin recovery, we are expected to learn how to be more open and honest about how we are feeling. Many men come into meetings scared to death, even though they're often unaware of how afraid they are. Rob, a twenty-seven-year-old financial advisor with five years of sobriety, commented on this:

Being a man in the Twelve Step program means that I have to be able to identify and reveal my feelings and secrets to other men. In our culture, men are often expected to keep their emotions and difficulties to themselves. Not only is the program itself challenging, but developing deeply emotional relationships adds to it.

Discovering our feelings in sobriety is an amazing process. Many men who are more "sensitive" have spent their lives feeling ashamed for having feelings and being teased, punished, and abused for showing them—first, by others; then, by themselves. Peter, a fifty-seven-year-old IT consultant with ten years of long-term recovery, said:

I spent an entire lifetime one way or another abusing some aspect of my behavior or my personality to avoid feeling. The only goal of my life was to not feel the way I did. Anything was better than feeling.

You may have felt this way, too. Is it any surprise, after years of keeping all of those feelings to ourselves and judging ourselves for having them, we would do everything in our power to avoid them?

We may have a difficult time admitting that we feel experiences in our lives deeply—given how most of us were raised, this doesn't seem to be a positive quality for men. Feelings seem to be the domain of women . . . at least that's the idea society has reinforced for almost two centuries now.[1] At most, we allow ourselves only certain emotions. Paul, a fifty-year-old service professional and union steward with twenty-four years of long-term recovery, said:

Before sobriety, I used to think I had only two feelings—anger and depression. Now I can really experience life and all of the emotions that go with it.

Jo, a fifty-nine-year-old pastor of a church for people in recovery, has fourteen years of long-term recovery. He talked about this issue at length:

Never let anyone know the real you. Never trust anyone to know what you are feeling unless it's a positive or a real masculine type of feeling such as "I've got control or power over this," "This isn't going to get me down," "I'll never run away," and so on. I can share those [kinds of] feelings easily. If I've got my shit together, then it's all good, but when I'm falling apart or when I'm really feeling vulnerable, afraid, or I don't have it under control . . . I could never share that.

What freedom you gain when you realize that being an emotional and sensitive man has nothing to do with your masculinity! Being sensitive is like having brown hair, brown eyes, or being six feet tall. You are not better or worse than anyone else. You are not any less of a man. Dan J., a thirty-eight-year-old architect with five years in sobriety, speaks to this issue poignantly:

I am a sensitive person. I feel things very strongly. I think the most important thing I have learned from my recovery is that it's okay for me to feel this way. I don't have to be tough to be a man. I can show my true feelings and still be okay. At the same time, I do not have to wear my emotions on my sleeve—not everything I feel is real.

Learning how to feel safe enough to experience our feelings and to not judge ourselves takes time. For some of us, the discovery of our feelings grows out of finally finding a safe and supportive environment to learn emotional awareness and to talk about how we feel.

Feelings Aren't Facts

Becoming aware of our feelings and developing the language to communicate them does present a danger of sorts:
we can begin to worship or get stuck in our feelings. When
Dan J. said "not everything I feel is real," he was referring to
the ways our feelings can dramatically affect our perception
of reality. Feelings are neither good nor bad; they simply are
what they are—emotions.

We learn in recovery that we are very accustomed to letting our emotions define our perception of the world. Even
though we are mostly unaware of them, our feelings affect
almost everything we do.

Sadly, our alienation from our feelings causes other problems. Most of us have long struggled with our emotional
awareness and how to acknowledge exactly what we are feeling without recognizing this. This struggle takes an immense
toll on our health, relationships, and quality of life. Before
recovery, we kept our feelings to ourselves, and we ended
up believing that only we felt such intense fear, inadequacy,
and loneliness. We let those feelings control our behavior
despite having no awareness of what was happening to us.
While we spent a lot of our time trying to control our emotions, in the end they controlled us. We hurt many people
because we rejected core parts of who we were. We did not
know how to take care of ourselves and meet our own needs.
Whether we were acting out in anger or isolating ourselves
in depression, we found ourselves caught in a vicious cycle:
because we felt unsafe and fearful, we responded with anger

and control. As a result, we frightened, hurt, and alienated those who cared about us. When we went to them looking for help and safety, they did not feel safe and were not able to comfort or help us. Not understanding the reasons for their response, we felt rejected and alone and we acted out again. And the cycle continued.

You can become lost in the discovery of your feelings and think that everything you do is related to how you feel. Once you are sober and working the Steps, you may find yourself flipping from one extreme to the other—from shut down and confused to an intense and uncontrolled expression of emotion.

Sometimes in recovery we let our feelings run our lives by using the excuse that we are addicts, or sensitive, or emotional when in fact we've experienced an inability to process our feelings. We've believed for years that feelings are bad and we are bad or weak for having them. As a result, we often simply don't know what we are feeling and spend much of our time reacting to life. Remember this—you are 100 percent responsible for how you respond to the events in your life. Yes, it's important that you allow yourself to feel, but don't let those feelings define how you live your life. Your emotional sensitivity is not an excuse for bad behavior.

I spent the first four years of my relationship with my partner unable to tell her when my feelings were hurt— which, as a sensitive (and somewhat immature) man, was quite often. Instead, I would feel hurt, take her actions personally, ascribe negative motives to them, feel alienated and shut off from her, and then turn my hurt into anger that I took out on her. Or, I would simply shut down and isolate in the basement. I responded similarly to much of my shame, fear, sadness, insecurity, and other feelings that I did not think I could express to her because they were not manly. Then, when I looked for a safe place to share how I was feeling, it was not to be found. I felt abandoned and unloved. Jo talked about this:

It's been a long-term process in therapy and in the Twelve Step program to discover how to get over my fear of intimacy and to share how I'm really feeling. I was in the program for a long time before I really came to grips with that—through divorces and failed relationships. I was sober but I was still very hesitant and reluctant to share who I was.

Charlie, a forty-five-year-old bus driver with twenty-three years of long-term recovery, talked about how he has learned to deal with his feelings:

I used to be a slave to my ever-changing emotions. Recovery has allowed me to stop running, to feel my feelings, and to learn that I've created them through my thoughts and choices. I lived as a victim to emotions and to the mental tapes that created them. Now my feelings are beloved guides that reveal my thinking and remind me I can choose again.

When you realize that consciously experiencing all of your feelings is okay, your life as a man will change because you will be able to be honest with yourself—about what you are really feeling.

Try not to force this process. Like everything in your recovery, let it happen. As the old AA saying goes, "Don't worry about getting in touch with your emotions; they will get in touch with you." Trust the process. Let others give you their support. Let the wise elders of recovery guide you. Share your feelings in meetings. Talk about them with your sponsor. Then, share them with the important people in your life in a spirit of intimacy—not in manipulation, blame, or an attempt to get someone to take care of you. If what you're feeling is really intense, it's especially advisable to give yourself some breathing room before you unload on someone and say something you might regret. Take some time to cool down; talk to a neutral party to get some perspective. Then, once you've sorted out what you're really reacting to, share your feelings with the relevant people.

Emotional Sobriety

Eventually you will realize that your recovery is limited unless it includes emotional sobriety. You are emotionally sober when you are aware of how you are feeling, able to express your feelings, able to be responsible for your feelings, able to respond and not overreact to those feelings, and to let them go. I have spoken to many men who, long into recovery, still feel hopeless about ever being able to truly feel good about themselves and their lives. They smile and tell you everything is great. They can quote the Steps and the literature. They know how to sound good. Yet they have not developed emotional sobriety. They are still little boys in men's bodies.

In *As Bill Sees It,* Bill Wilson talked about emotional sobriety:

If we examine every disturbance we have, great or small, we will find at the root of it some unhealthy dependency and its consequent unhealthy demand. Let us, with God's help, continually surrender these hobbling liabilities. Then we can be set free to live and love; we may be able to twelfth-step ourselves, as well as others, into emotional sobriety.[2]

Rich, a former lawyer with seven years of sobriety, said:

The change for me today is that I can more accurately recognize my feelings. In the past, fear, grief, or pain was usually masked by a veneer of anger, but today I can more often identify the actual emotion or feeling that is in play.

The process of discovering our feelings often proceeds like this: First, we become aware that we have feelings. Next, we learn how to talk about our feelings, a more intellectual process. For me, that meant talking about feeling hurt and afraid while coming across as angry or while laughing when I spoke. While I could correctly identify a given feeling, my behavior didn't match. Next, we learn to actually feel the feeling and identify that feeling. We learn how to express and feel all our emotions including pain, sadness, fear, and shame. Finally, we learn how to experience our feelings in the moment and let them pass through us. Men in this stage of awareness are living in the moment, unafraid to express how they feel. The process of getting there is often messy, and we will make mistakes. Thankfully we have the Steps to guide us, and we have our recovery community of both men and women and our Higher Power to show us the way!

STEP ONE

We admitted we were powerless over alcohol—
that our lives had become unmanageable.

When I grew up, I learned two things
about what it takes to be a man.
Number one, I learned to fight and
number two, I learned to drink.

– JO –

The following statement begins the discussion of Step One in the book *Twelve Steps and Twelve Traditions*: "Who cares to admit complete defeat? Practically no one, of course. Every natural instinct cries out against the idea of personal powerlessness."[1] As men, feeling powerless is the opposite of feeling in control, and from a very early age as a man, you were probably taught (though you didn't realize it) that you should try to be the master of your world as best you could. Brandon said:

> *Powerlessness at first seems to be unmanly. In fact, I don't know*
> *if I see powerlessness ever to be manly, but it doesn't bother*
> *me now to lack that manly quality. The first three Steps have*

challenged my desire for manliness in general. It's about com-ing to terms with self and being okay with having it clash with stereotyped manliness.

When I was writing my master's thesis, in which I looked at masculinity in the Twelve Step community, a friend brought me a magazine ad. In the ad was a very masculine arm out-stretched with the palm open ready to shake the reader's hand. There was a bottle of liquor neatly tucked in at the bottom of the page. The caption read: Get in touch with your masculine side. The message was clear: real men drink. Another message could easily be inferred, too: if you do not drink alcohol, you are not a real man. And so, when you stand at the cliff of despair because your use of alcohol and other drugs has gotten out of control, you face not just the foreign territory of sobriety but very possibly surrendering a core concept of your masculinity.

Everywhere in our culture we see and hear messages like this that tell us what it means to be a man, and nearly all of them are the opposite of what Step One teaches us. Following is an example:

Being a man = *The consumption of alcohol*
Believing "Real men don't get out of control" coupled
  with "Real men know how to party" (i.e., get drunk)
Believing men are powerful
Believing men are in control
Keeping your thoughts and feelings to yourself

*Always keeping up a good front—"never let them see
you sweat"*
*Being fiercely independent; relationships are not a
priority*

Being a man ≠ *The absence of alcohol*
Embracing powerlessness and acceptance
Letting go of control
*Admitting or confessing—allowing yourself to be
known to another; unmanageability*
*Being part of the group and in close relationship
with others*

Each of these concepts is explored in Step One, though
you may not recognize them or use the same words to
describe them. Step One—admitting powerlessness and
unmanageability—may not seem like a very manly Step to
you. It may surprise you to hear, though, that Step One will
actually enhance your ability to live your life as powerfully
as possible. Brian, a psychiatrist with twenty-one years of
sobriety said it very well:

*Admitting and accepting powerlessness at face value challenges
the notion that men are strong, self-sufficient, and should not
admit weakness. Paradoxically, recognizing and admitting powerlessness takes incredible courage and honesty, and is more manly
than living in the fantasy world of denial.*

The word *powerless* often has a negative connotation.
Being powerless over alcohol and other drugs means that

you are unable to control what happens to you when you put these substances in your body. (While I reference alcohol and other drugs throughout this book, I encourage you to apply these principles and ideas to whatever addiction you are struggling with and whatever Twelve Step community you are a part of at this time.) We've all tried to control our addiction. We've made statements such as, "I need to cut back" or "I just need to moderate." "Maybe just drink beer." "Only smoke pot." "Snort cocaine, but not inject it." "Look at porn only once a day." "Eat only twice a day." How many people have told you to cut back? Your attempts to control your addiction failed, and now you find yourself in a strange new situation.

Addiction to alcohol and other drugs is a cunning and baffling brain disease, which the founders of AA were quite aware of, if only intuitively, many decades ago. They were also aware of the physical (allergy) and mental (obsession) components of the disease:

> . . . Once he takes any alcohol whatever into his system, something happens, both in the bodily and mental sense, which makes it virtually impossible for him to stop . . . These observations would be pointless if our friend never took the first drink, thereby setting the terrible cycle in motion. Therefore, the main problem of the alcoholic centers in his mind, rather than in his body.[2]

Throughout your sobriety you will face that insane urge to use. Much of this urge is caused by the physical impact that alcohol and other drugs have had on your body, particularly your brain. You will face numerous times in your life when you contemplate giving up on some part of your recovery, or on your recovery as a whole. When you have been successful in the past, it's because you refused to give up. You were powerful—not power*less!* This quality of perseverance—a valuable quality that is traditionally considered masculine—will ultimately serve you in your recovery.

But taken to an extreme, this character trait of fierce determination and "no retreat, no surrender!" tells you that if you admit defeat you are not a man. Chances are you have fought the good fight with your addiction. You have tried everything you could think of. But now you must accept the reality that defeat is okay, and that it doesn't mean you're any less of a man. Instead, by admitting defeat and surrendering, you win. Out of defeat comes victory.

Once you have admitted that you are powerless over your addiction, you will see that you have the power to work the Steps and recover. Step One gives you the opportunity to see the areas of your life in which you have no power and those in which you do. Knowing the difference—the essence of the Serenity Prayer[3]—is critical to finding happiness in your recovery. For example, you do not have power over the inevitable cravings to use again—no matter how much you try. But you do have the power to go to a meeting or pick up the phone and call your sponsor when those cravings kick in. The better your understanding of this difference, the more powerful you will be. The more you can approach powerlessness without judgment and emotion, the more you will be able to accept the many people, places, and things you can't control.

From Powerlessness to Acceptance

Some of us coming into recovery are all too familiar with feeling powerless. Many of us come from abusive backgrounds where the experience of powerlessness was literally beaten into us as children. Any attempt to find power today could reinforce how powerless you felt as a child. That pain may also explode into your awareness, and you'll find yourself reacting in ways that surprise or shock you. On the other hand, you may believe that the way you were treated was acceptable, that you deserved what you got, or that this was just how boys are supposed to be raised. Accepting and even embracing powerlessness is a delicate Step, and one that promises clarity. Getting care from a professional would be a good healing step to take.

Larry, who has twenty years of sobriety and is a professional psychologist, offered another way of talking about powerlessness. Larry believes admitting you are powerless is essentially the deep acceptance of a situation. If the word *powerless* bothers you, think of it as *acceptance*—a more neutral word. At some point, you will learn what you cannot control, and you will be able to take responsibility for those things you can change.

Once you can get past the idea that powerlessness and acceptance somehow challenge your manhood, you can begin to see the wisdom of powerlessness and acceptance in many of your day-to-day interactions. Are you worried about how a coworker perceives your job performance? Remind yourself that you are powerless over what other people think.

Complaining about your job and its lack of adequate pay? Accept that you cannot change your situation right now, get back to work, and make a plan for addressing the issue. As Kit said, "I need to always remember that though I am powerless, I am not helpless." And Jo said:

> You don't need the Steps if you have the power to take care of something . . . If you don't have the power—then work the Steps.

A man in one of my meetings always prefaced his comments by saying: "My name is Rich, and I am powerless and with the help of my Higher Power I am truly empowered, and for that I am grateful."

Power, Privilege, and Entitlement

> **I have trouble separating my strong sense of being special as a person from my deeply rooted sense of being special because I am a man.**
>
> - D A V E -

We need to understand how our culture views power in order to understand powerlessness in our recovery and relationships. Most power in Western societies is power over someone or something—a masculine form of power. We can also think of power as power with or power for—a more feminine expression. Most professional offices are organized with masculine power structure—a hierarchy with one person having control and power over his or her staff. The service structure of Twelve Step communities is based on a more feminine concept of power in which individual members are accountable to the group conscience. Neither type of power is better than the other, and both have a place in our lives.

Few men in our culture were raised to understand or use much of anything feminine, let alone a feminine type of power. Men are supposed to have power over everything . . . or so we think. Before recovery, most of us tried to apply masculine power—the only kind we were "allowed" to use—to every area of our lives. The results were far from effective.

Using masculine power, or "power over," in your personal relationships doesn't work particularly well. No one wants to be treated as inferior. People may do what we want but only out of fear of our reaction or, at the extreme, fear for their safety. Sometimes we use power to get what we think we deserve or are owed—to be taken care of or waited on, for example. Do you expect your partner to take care of you? Do you use a raised voice, criticism, or even violence to force your partner into doing what you want done? How has this affected your relationships?

At this point you may be saying, "No matter how I act on the outside, I still don't feel at all powerful. I have spent most of my life trying to feel strong and powerful, but instead I've felt abandoned, unloved, and rejected in every relationship I've had." Brian talked about this exact concern:

This is a hard topic for someone who has faced as much insecurity and self-doubt during life as I have. For much of it, I have felt that I've been undeserving of things because I was not man enough.

Brian's comments lead us to still more questions: How do you act when you are afraid of being abandoned, of being unloved, or rejected? Who is responsible for your situation? I used to spend so much time focusing on how I felt that I never noticed how I was treating others.

As long as you are using your power to control and dominate your relationships, you will never have the closeness and love you seek. Remember, you are 100 percent responsible for the way you treat others. Treat others badly and your relationships will not give you what you're looking for, and you'll feel sad, frustrated, angry, and afraid as a result. If you want to have more loving relationships, love. As the saying goes, "as you give, so shall you receive." If you can't do this on your own, get help. If you choose not to, know that the consequences you experience are always the result of the choices you make.

Recovery offers you the chance to experience true and appropriate power—power that is not used to control or frighten others. Without specifically addressing masculine or feminine power, Quinn talked about how his experience with power has changed as a result of his involvement in AA:

> When I was young, I thought of power as additive. By that I mean the more I took, the more I had. Kind of like money. The program has helped me see that the more I take, the less I have. Being powerful enough to experience my powerlessness is being awake and fully alive.

Because You're a Man

Have you ever thought you deserved special treatment just because you're a man? Have you ever received special treatment just because you're a guy? Chances are you have whether or not you realized it. The special treatment we're talking about is related to two important concepts we'll be exploring next: privilege and entitlement. Privilege is the benefit you get from society simply because you are a man. Entitlement, in Twelve Step language, is a destructive defect of character. We experience entitlement when we believe we have a right to certain things and privileges, and that our needs are more important than the needs of others.

The Privilege Not to See

Those who benefit from privilege rarely recognize the privileges they have. For example, how often do you think about the fact that you are highly unlikely to be a victim of sexual assault? Most men don't come to this awareness on their own. I didn't realize that I never really thought about sexual assault until I sat in a college class and heard women talk about their fear of, or experience with, rape and sexual abuse. Quinn, who has worked hard to look at these issues, said:

Of course I feel privileged. Every time I walk down the street unafraid of being mugged or raped, I feel privileged.

Larry talked about a wake-up call that came in one of his AA meetings:

My home group was a noon meeting with a number of women. The safety I felt allowed me to really hear what their experience in recovery was like. I heard and saw the effects of abuse, most of it done by men. I began to see the effects of power over others and that I was someone with that same power just because I was a male.

You can often express yourself differently than women, whether in public or private. Dave touched on this idea when he said:

> *I feel comfortable talking loudly, taking up physical space without asking, and speaking over someone else. My behavior is often tolerated because I am a man.*

What advantages or benefits do you see yourself having just because you're male? What privileges have you been given over the years because you're a man?

Sexism

The term *sexism* is emotionally charged for many men. It often raises defenses (and shame), and we often simply ignore the issue. We do so, in part, simply because we can. We're being sexist, for example, when we act as though what we say, think, value, and do is more important than what women say, think, value, or do—just because we're men. One way some boys and men make fun of one another is to use derogatory feminine names or phrases. Think about these insults: "Sissy!" "You throw like a girl!" "Pussy!" "Momma's boy!" Masculinity is often defined as anything "not feminine." What message about girls and women do such insults give to boys? How do you think they affect the way girls and women think of themselves? The message that women are somehow less than men, or little more than a sex object for men, is still commonly found in our society. You may think that there's no reason for you, as a guy, to pay attention to such stereotyping, but you do. We all do because those messages influence how *we* think about, value, relate to, and care for girls and women in our lives.

Men seldom hold one other accountable regarding how we talk about or act toward women. We may hide hurt and confusion from past and present relationships with women behind sexist comments. As Dan J. said:

In recovery, most of my prejudices have been reduced or have disappeared. I try to be open-minded when it comes to these issues. Sexism is still my biggest defect of character. I have been working at understanding how my resentments toward my mother affect my relationships with women.

You are not necessarily a bad person if you have sexist attitudes. Perhaps this is the first time you've ever examined these attitudes. But here's the question to ask yourself: do they represent or reflect the man you want to be now . . . in recovery?

Homophobia

Homophobia is deeply rooted within many men in many cultures. Dan J. spoke about some of his experiences in the military. "I saw two medics get beat up for allegedly being gay and two cooks outcast for sharing a bunk after a wild night of partying." We often live a rigid masculine life—doing everything we can to not be too emotional or affectionate with other men.

Dave talked about how he has grown as a result of sponsoring gay men:

I learned that their struggles with romantic relationships are strikingly similar to my own. I also became more aware of the pressure of being a gay man in a homophobic culture. I found myself listening to my jokes differently and staying quiet more often when opportunities to label other men and their behaviors as gay arose.

Why, when we want to make fun of boys and men who are emotional or who express affection for one another, do we imply that they are homosexuals? Why is that even considered an insult? Are gay guys the only men who have feelings or express their emotions? Hardly. We've already talked about how many men view expressions of emotion as feminine or weak. By implying that gays aren't real men because of this, we're both belittling women and reinforcing the negative stereotype of men as hard, unfeeling, and cold.

Try for a moment to imagine what it's like to live as a gay man in a world of men who don't accept who you are, and dislike or even hate you for it. Gary said he did not feel entitlement as a gay man:

Even though I am a man, I am a gay man, and being a gay man is the worst of both worlds. I am seen as a predator, weak, dangerous, sick, and as the "other" all at once by the same people.

Imagine how you'd feel if in every meeting you attended everyone assumed you were gay and all of the topics focused on gay relationships and sex? What if every time you went out to fellowship all of the men made fun of straight guys and pretended to be straight in disparaging ways? Imagine this happening a lot! It's more likely, of course, that nothing like this will ever happen to you—and again, that is privilege. So again, ask yourself whether your judgments, beliefs, and behaviors represent the person—the man—you want to be in recovery.

A Solution to the Inequities of Entitlement and Privilege

The Twelve Steps can be part of the solution. Below are a few examples of ways you can see how these issues play out in your life:

- *Read about entitlement and privilege, and talk to other men whom you respect.*
- *Do Step Four inventories about how you treat gays and women.*
- *Talk to women about your experiences—and theirs.*
- *Volunteer at a domestic violence shelter or a domestic abuse program.*
- *Speak up in meetings or fellowship when you see unacceptable behavior or hear unacceptable comments.*
- *Lovingly confront men who are being homophobic or sexist.*
- *Reach out to gay men, and help them to feel comfortable in meetings.*
- *Notice your language—do not use "chick," "bitch," and "girl" or other belittling words when speaking about women.*
- *Pray for guidance, and ask each day for increased awareness.*

Juan talked about using the Steps to deal with these issues and how he came to peace with his brothers' homosexuality:

I found a real acceptance of who they are and [how they've] been freed of the fear of the stigma of homosexuality. In the early days, their homosexuality threatened my masculinity. I used to think that because they were homosexuals, then I had to be one as well.

Juan has since made amends to both of his brothers. He talked, too, about making amends for his behavior toward women, his old girlfriend in particular:

I had no business being a part of her life. At the advice of my sponsor, I wrote a letter to God and made a donation to a battered woman's shelter.

Miguel talked about recovery allowing him to let go of the fear of being less of a man or being perceived as gay, a defect of character that haunts a lot of men long into their recovery:

I look at flowers and I think they are pretty. Is that okay? It is now. I like flowers. I've been watching this dance show—the athleticism is awesome and the talent is incredible. Would I have been caught watching that show back when I was drinking? Even if I liked it, I doubt it.

Every man I spoke with in writing this book told me that he is more comfortable with himself and cares less what other people—especially men—think about him.

Juan now understands the important role women must play in our growth:

Women need to be a part of this or we are in big trouble. They can help us evolve.

You are responsible for looking at how these issues affect your life and the lives of those you love. Remember that you are not alone. If you ask, help is available. It may not be with your sponsor or in the meetings you go to—but you will find what you need. As Larry said:

I'm mindful of privilege. If I don't address my power and privilege issues, I run the risk of discounting other people's experiences.

Certainly this is in line with the principles of AA. Maybe it should be written somewhere that the only requirement for membership is the desire to be human.

Unmanageability

Step One also addresses the idea of unmanageability. Unmanageability means that because of the destructive impact of alcohol and other drugs you are not doing the best job of running your life. Do you believe that you are the one who should be guiding your life? Does it feel like an assignment you have always had? You can't protect the women-folk and children if your life is unmanageable, right? You can't be a man if you are not in charge . . . right? Or can you?

Here is one of recovery's wonderful paradoxes: life is manageable so long as you recognize its unmanageability. By accepting the unmanageability of your life, you will be able to accomplish much, creating a life you never dreamed possible. You will have a greater sense of peace knowing that you don't have to be life's manager. Instead, you can be the worker bee and follow life's guidance one day at a time.

We

The first word in Step One is *we,* one of the most powerful and significant words in all of the Twelve Steps for men in recovery. Men are great at acting as if we are part of the crowd, especially when we are using. We can be the life of the party once we have enough social lubricant inside of us. But at the same time, we can never fully escape our feelings of loneliness. Take away the drugs, and we find ourselves struggling to connect with others. We are not sure how to be a part of the group without drugs propping us up.

Most of us were not raised to see ourselves as part of a larger community—the We. Even in our closest relationships, we often had much difficulty being part of the We. The Twelve Step community would say it is almost impossible to live disconnected from others and stay sober. West, a forty-two-year-old with twenty years of sobriety and the CEO of a national organization, refers to the Twelve Step community as "The Tribe." As members of The Tribe, we always belong, and we get what we need when we ask for it. Dave's words reflect the power of The Tribe to heal a man's loneliness:

As fate would have it, there was a conference in a neighboring town. I dragged my pain along to the event. Arriving early to a meeting, I sat alone in my sorrow. Soon, the sound of AA happiness penetrated my self-inflicted exile. I looked around just at the point when the 3,000 people were joining hands to open the meeting with the Serenity Prayer. God sent the voices of 3,000 other alcoholics to answer my fear of loneliness.

Thanks to the guidance and wisdom of Step One, we get to reconnect—really connect—with the other people in our lives. We learn that others can help comfort the wounds created by our addiction and the absence of the drugs. We do not have to experience powerlessness in isolation. We can let others get close to us and help us.

When we sit in the rooms with one another and are joined by the elders of The Tribe and hear men talking about both their struggles and the progress they are making, we sit in a circle of profound fellowship. We are given hope that we, too, can succeed in this journey.

The We of the program is also our valuable and incredible connection to humanity. Suddenly, The Tribe has the possibility of being as big as we wish it to be. I have heard the common bond of recovery spoken by men from all over the world—Ireland, Mexico, Russia, India, China, and more. It's amazing to realize that the man who is sponsoring you can trace his AA roots back to 1935 when two men in Akron, Ohio, were desperately searching for a way out of their own suffering. Imagine that the men who you will sponsor will sponsor other men who in turn will sponsor others many decades from now. Incredible, isn't it? The founders of AA were neither saints nor heroes; they were just two men talking to each other about recovery, staying sober the best they could, and passing that message on to others. Today, that message encircles our planet.

Do You Want to Live, or Do You Want to Die?

Maybe this is an exaggeration, but an old-timer I know, when talking about Step One, said that at the end of the day your sobriety comes down to life and death: do you want to live, or do you want to die? Men are raised to fantasize about our self-destruction—to burn out rather than fade away; to laugh in the face of death. Well, staring death in the face is not nearly as romantic as the movies make it seem. Chris, a thirty-one-year-old artist with nine years of sobriety, talked about his experience with Step One:

I knew for a long time that I was a mess, and I knew that I was going to commit suicide. I didn't understand that this was the disease talking until much later when it almost killed my mother. Tragically, it's still slowly killing my father, and it almost killed me. I didn't know addiction was so powerful—that it ruins lives and families. The first step for me was realizing that I didn't know what the hell the First Step was! At some point, I just knew I wanted to stay alive . . . that's what the First Step is—do you want to live or not?

I have been in recovery long enough to have buried two sponsees and attended many more funerals of others I have known in recovery—many died sober and others as a result of relapse. Every time a member of the recovery community dies, his death reminds those of us who are paying attention that our sobriety is very grave business indeed and should not be taken lightly. Your sobriety is not to be taken for granted regardless of how many years in the program you might have. Once you have been sober for a while, it may be difficult to remember how bad your life had been when you were still using. The out-of-control using. The paranoia. The suicidal thoughts. The alienation, depression, and anxiety. Remember those experiences. You will meet men who tell of years—even decades—spent sober, who relapse and self-destruct. We have to remember how bad our lives could be again if we stop taking care of ourselves. Addiction is the disease, sobriety is the medicine, and the Twelve Steps are the spoonful of sugar that helps the medicine go down. Like other chronic diseases such as diabetes, addiction requires constant maintenance and attention. You are never cured! Eventually, though, taking care of yourself becomes a natural part of your life. Monitoring your stress level, the biggest trigger for any addict, becomes the essential practice of your life.

As Chris points out, Step One is essentially saying, "I do not want to die. I give up. I surrender." As if admitting this reality isn't hard enough, who would actually choose to live in a way that may seem rather unmanly? A man who chooses life. The remaining Steps are the solution because they show us how to live—that's why they're often referred to as a design for living. By living them, you'll discover what masculine power really is.

Always a Newcomer

Every man in recovery faces a critical danger: losing touch with being a newcomer. Think of the desperation and excitement so many of us feel early in our recovery. Everything is new. We don't know much about how to stay sober, let alone how to live, but our minds are open and the pain is raw. But after six months or so, we don't want to be seen as a newcomer at all. We talk confidently about how we have worked all twelve of the Steps, and we refer to our first month in recovery as "back when I was new"—as if we now have all of the answers. We don't like not having answers. We don't like being newcomers because we're low man on the ladder—or so we think.

West was struck by a simple truth he rediscovered as he began working the Steps again. "I am a flawed human being," he said. West laughs when he remembers how humbling it feels to notice fear, judgment, or any of the other bedevilments that still arise in him on a daily basis at twenty years sober:

It is who I am and there is nothing wrong with that. The danger is losing sight of this fact. The danger is thinking that I am somehow normal or cured. Things do not go well for me when I think that way, and it has taken me twenty years to learn this. There is freedom in admitting this on a daily basis. Every day that starts with this admission is a day when I am freer in all of my relationships.

In the end, if you lose touch with what it means to be a newcomer, if you forget that you are always a newcomer because you will always have more to learn, then you won't be able to learn what Step One can teach you. West continued, "It is amazing—twenty years later and everything that kept me sober is what keeps me sober today." As you mature in your recovery day by day, week by week, and year by year, you will learn that the surrender of Step One is the foundation of recovery—and of life. You have the opportunity to surrender on a daily basis. As it unfolds, each moment is an opportunity for surrender. You do not know what that moment will bring or where it will take you. Hence, you are always a newcomer because life is always new. You come to each moment new, and you have no answers. That is Step One. That is freedom.

STEP TWO

*Came to believe that a Power greater than ourselves
could restore us to sanity.*

**When I came into the program of AA,
I had a little tiny God, now I have an
awesome powerful God that I listen to
and do my best to "pray" attention to.**

- JOE P. -

As men, many of us struggle with the concept of a Higher
Power when we first begin recovery. You may call it Love,
Truth, Nature, or Higher Self. You may have experienced it
as Money, Sex, Drugs, or Fame. Regardless of how you name
it—this power greater than you has been with you throughout your life, though perhaps with different faces. The Big
Book tells us:

> . . . *For deep down in every man, woman, and child, is the funda-
> mental idea of God. It may be obscured by calamity, by pomp, by
> worship of other things, but in some form or other it is there.*[1]

The key is realizing that, whatever this power is, *you* are
not it. Juan talked about some guidance he received when

he first got sober: "Early on, my response to Step Two, with the help of a crusty old junkie friend, was 'anything other than self.'"

As you develop your relationship with your Higher Power, try not to do what we men have a strong tendency to do—treat this Step as only an intellectual decision. When Step Two is an intellectual decision or an item on a checklist, guess who often ends up playing the part of the Higher Power? You! You might give the Higher Power lip-service, but you are still the one in control—as proven by your thinking process and behaviors. An instructive joke from Twelve Step meetings goes as follows: "What is the only difference between me and God? God never pretends to be me." On one level, you are probably aware of many powers greater than you (your boss, traffic, the weather). Our modern world is based on the illusion that we can successfully control our lives and the lives of those around us, which in essence is playing the role of the Higher Power. How much of your life have you spent trying to be your own Higher Power without realizing it?

Believing in a power greater than ourselves hits at the core of our masculinity. As men, so much of our lives are spent trying to analyze problems, and we expect to have the answers—all of them! It's common for our male egos to take a big hit when we have to admit that we cannot do everything on our own—that we do not know everything. Casey spoke about this:

We all like to solve our own problems, and we think we should be able to do this on our own. The idea of getting help and of a Higher Power didn't exist in my life until I got into recovery.

Dave talked about his attitude toward life before recovery, "I thought that my own resources of will and intellect would be enough to navigate me out of my problems." But they weren't! Like Dave, many of us are convinced that the expectation that we use our ability to think and solve our problems is not just an unwritten law—it's essential to our survival. Stop for a moment and think. Do you believe you have to have all of the answers? What does it mean if you don't have them? How hard is it for you to ask for help? What feelings, thoughts, and reactions does the idea of a power greater than you bring up?

Tear Down the Wall

Do you remember any times when you experienced a power greater than you? Were they positive? Think about your childhood and try to remember how you felt when you knew you were not alone and had someone to take care of you.

Some of your memories of a power greater than you may be of adults, siblings, or other kids who were harsh, violent, or overwhelming. Your father? Mother? Your older brothers? The school bully? The "popular" kids? Those experiences may have reinforced your feelings of powerlessness. They may have led you to believe that your Higher Power was letting this happen. When we encounter such difficulties, sometimes we try desperately to keep ourselves safe. We decide that we are the only power we can trust. Juan's comments at eight years old as a result of the pain from his parents' divorce are telling: "I remember saying 'I will never let anyone hurt me again.' I remember [creating] a wall."

Oftentimes we create public personas or masks to protect us from the world—that's part of the "wall" Juan referred to. These personas might help us when we are younger, but they often cause problems for us when we are older. Shutting down our feelings or using walls to keep others from getting close is what we face in Step Two. The question is, are you willing to remove those walls and trust again?

Our confused or mistaken thinking says: if we ask for help, we will look weak, and we can't look weak and be men— at least not "real" men. As a result, we learn to ignore our insecurity, fear, and doubt. Rather than show these feelings, we present an image to the world that we have everything under control.

Step Two can help you create a relationship with a power greater than you, but first you have to remove the obstacles blocking that relationship. First, try to take an honest look at the current state of your life and consider these questions: Are you ready to try another way of living? Are you willing to let go of how you think men are supposed to live if it means that your life will get better? Are you willing to believe in a power greater than you?

A New Kind of Man

When we begin to develop a relationship with a Higher Power, something begins to happen to us as men. We begin to experience masculinity in a new way. As a man, your loss of connection to your Higher Power may have been related to your rejection of your feelings and sensitivity. This rejection, as we talked about earlier, seems to be a requirement to being accepted as a man in much of our society. Many of us were taught or even forced to surrender these qualities. Perhaps you can relate to Juan's remarks:

I was always very sensitive, but I didn't see that as being something positive or good. I got teased quite a bit. I hated to be made fun of.

Many of us share Juan's feelings and experience. We disconnected from ourselves, from others, and in some ways, from life itself. As a result, we eventually became increasingly isolated and lonely. We created more walls, and we created more masks to wear. Eventually, we came into recovery where we were told that if we do not get honest about our fears, our insecurities, and the problems in our lives, we will not stay sober. "Take off the masks! Tear down the walls!" they say. But how?

I remember listening to a guy in one of my first meetings who looked like a true man's man—a burly guy wearing a sweat-stained white T-shirt and faded blue jeans with a beer gut. But he talked about how afraid he was! I had never heard a man talk about fear—let alone in front of a group! Dave talked at length about how his ideas about men changed when he got into recovery:

I was accustomed to hearing men talk about sports and sex and drinking stories. But after meetings, I'd hear men discuss the value of applying prayer to the difficulties in their lives. They discussed how a relationship with God provided relief from their

pain and strength to endure their problems and to solve them . . .
I suddenly found myself believing that I could benefit from having
a relationship with God.

Dave will tell you that the man he is today is due to the relationship he developed with his Higher Power. This relationship has not only given him permission to acknowledge his problems and seek help for them—but he now sees that process as one of his great strengths.

Other men in recovery can give us permission to acknowledge those parts of our lives that were always there, and they show us how to do that by their example. Reggie told me a wonderful story about the transformation of his relationship with his God—and his life:

While a life-long Christian, I nevertheless struggled with my belief
in God and wondered privately about God's very existence. I was
unconvinced that God really cared about me or could be there for
me, especially then, when I needed Him most.

Reggie went on to talk about how, eighteen months into his recovery, he had to face some difficult truths that he had been hiding, including two DWIs and six years of delinquent taxes. The men in his Twelve Step meetings, and especially his sponsor, were telling him that he needed to face these problems in order to maintain his sobriety:

I learned a lot about Higher Powers when I became a Twelve
Step group member. Did God really want me to go to jail? The
inner turmoil was unbearable. I turned myself in for the first of
two DWI offenses. My worst fears were not realized. I was made
to pay a fine and serve probation before judgment. I was told that
the charge would disappear from my record if I did not repeat

the offense. One by one, I mustered the courage, with the help of my sponsor and my Higher Power, to face each of my infractions. What I learned was clear—the fear was much worse than the consequence. Ironically, the IRS owed me money, and I got a small, but unexpected refund once all of my returns were filed! Was this God working in my life?

Like Reggie, you may be keeping certain secrets or believe that you have problems that your Higher Power cannot help you with. You may think that you are beyond help. Or, you may be ashamed to admit your fear or insecurity or the problems that tear your life apart. When you share those problems with your group, you share them with your Higher Power. When you let the group and your Higher Power help, you become a new and different kind of man.

Restore Us to Sanity

The second part of Step Two talks about being restored to sanity. We can easily limit our understanding of the concept of insanity to that of being crazy and having crazy thoughts. Certainly we've committed some pretty insane acts in our addiction and even after beginning recovery. In the Twelve Step community, we define *insanity* as a lack of wholeness or a feeling of intense disconnection from others, from ourselves, and from our Higher Power.

In early sobriety, it may seem to you that finding wholeness is impossible. Charlie thought of some of the harmful acts he committed in his addiction. He blinded a man by throwing a piece of metal off a bridge. He set fires to homes. With that past following him into recovery, he said, "I did not believe that I could be restored to health—I was convinced that I was defective and bad."

Dave was talking about Step Two, insanity, and believing in a power greater than oneself when he said:

I didn't like the idea of insanity. To me I thought it was an admission of brokenness.

For Dave, being broken is a lot harder to address than not being whole. When you are broken, you require fixing. When you lack wholeness you require community and support.

When you begin to share the new person, the new man, you're becoming with your recovery community, you do not have to pretend to have your life together. Acknowledging your disconnection and isolation becomes a gateway to wholeness. Brian talked about this idea of disclosure. He said, "Where the Step says our Higher Power is restoring us to sanity, to me that means that as an individual we cannot restore ourselves to sanity, and that idea once again challenges the idea of self-sufficiency." This restoration has to be done in community.

Group of Drunks

Working our program and going to meetings will always bring us back to our Higher Power. At some point in your sobriety, you may have feelings of despair, that there's nothing good in the world, or that no Higher Power would care about you. That's exactly the time to let the Twelve Step community itself be your Higher Power. The meetings can be your lifeline back to society and sanity; there are other men, like you, who have "solved the drink problem" and who can and will help you.

It doesn't matter whether or not you believe in God if you are plugged into the Twelve Step community. In it you automatically have an incredibly effective power greater than you. In discussing Step Two in meetings, you'll probably hear people say that G.O.D. for them simply stands for a "Group of Drunks" or "Good Orderly Direction." West said it well:

All I know is I still have a lot of "stuff" with the whole God concept left over from how I grew up. It has been difficult for me to shake. I have full faith in the power of the group. It is the God piece that gets in the way for me. So I decided that until I get the God stuff worked out, I will trust in the power of the recovery community.

You can come to believe that you are safe enough with your recovery group to share your hurt and your pain with them. You can find acceptance with them despite any unacceptable acts you have committed. With their help, you come to believe that the insanity in which you have been living can disappear.

Out of your insanity can come a wonderful and surprising new connection to other men in the program—and to your Higher Power. You may not have learned this as a child, but wise men know they cannot go through life alone. In time, you begin to really trust that turning to your Higher Power will restore you to sanity, and in turn you come to believe, despite all evidence to the contrary, that no matter what happens, all is well with the world.

All Is Well

Many of the men I interviewed talked about admitting powerlessness and believing in a power greater than oneself. They spoke of the insecurity they felt at first. With your admission of powerlessness, Step Two can help you have a relationship with a power greater than you and access the power that you need to thrive in the world. You may, however, still find yourself wanting to fall back into control—or what you thought was control! For millennia, however, sages, mystics, and all the others who pay attention to life have come to a simple conclusion: "All is well."

Life sometimes feels as though it's falling apart for one very simple reason—because it is. In fact, life is constantly falling apart, and then offering us the opportunity to experience the full depth of what it means to be human. When you are settled with deep faith in the inherent goodness of the universe, invite your life to fall apart. You will be okay. You will be okay because "all is well."

This idea is difficult for many men to embrace. "Do you mean I am not in charge?" Yes, exactly. "I do not have to fix everything?" No, you do not have to hold all of the pieces in place. All you need is to believe and trust. No matter how your outside life is arranged. No matter how crazy the world seems. No matter how much it seems as though the dark side has won. No matter how you feel. "All is well."

All will be well because all has always been well. Whether or not you remember or believe this essential Truth of Life does not matter. The Truth does not depend on you to be the Truth. And that Truth is the essence of Step Two. The essence of life. No matter where you are in the program, or how long you have been sober, you will always come back to Step Two. I cannot say how many times over the years my sponsor, Eric, said:

> *You have not worked Step Two, Dan. You have no faith that everything is going to be okay. You need to go back to Step Two.*

While your experience with Step Two may have started with recognition of a power greater than you, it blossoms into faith, then a belief, and then a knowing that tells you no matter what, "all is well."

$\dot{\mathbf{Y}}$

STEP THREE

*Made a decision to turn our will and our lives
over to the care of God,* as we understood Him.

**Look at what we grew up with.
We have the Marlboro man . . . and the
ultimate "I can do it myself" image . . .
John Wayne and Clint Eastwood . . .
Just by force of will we control and
dominate everything around us.**

– PETER –

So how do men practice Step Three—turning your will
and life over to your Higher Power—when we have been
taught for so long to exert our will and control? In Step One
you learned about powerlessness and what real power is.
In Step Two, you acknowledged a Higher Power's existence
and accepted that it can help you—in other words, restore
you to sanity. Acknowledging that someone or something
can help you, and actually reaching out for that help, are
two very different actions. In Step Three, you do not just accept that a Higher Power can help you—you also reach out

and ideally even embrace the help. Reaching out for help may not come easily to you, nor does it for many men in our culture, so you may not feel particularly comfortable doing so. At least not at first. Here's a typical response: "Okay, I acknowledged that I needed help with my drug use. But I am fine now. Do you know how hard I have had to work to try to convince everyone that I do not need any more help? I'm fine; now I'll take care of the rest!"

Why Not Choose Your Own Higher Power?

Right from the start, many of us get stuck as we try to define our Higher Power—one of our most important and valuable sources of help. Step Three opens an incredible door, for there are not five more important words in the Twelve Step recovery culture than these: "God, *as you understood Him.*" This is your chance to define your Higher Power. For many of us who grew up with the Christian God, a Higher Power was unreachable and untouchable. What's more, one could never be so arrogant as to define God in your own way!

In Step Three, you realize that you can personalize your relationship with your Higher Power—first by getting rid of the idea that you have to call it "God" or need to join a religion. In a wonderful excerpt from the book *As Bill Sees It,* Bill writes in one of his many letters:

> *We are only operating a spiritual kindergarten in which people are enabled to get over drinking and find the grace to go on living to better effect. Each man's theology has to be his own quest, his own affair.*[1]

Quinn, who spent many years in the seminary before ultimately leaving to become a therapist, said:

I have great faith but almost no beliefs. My religious training was about belief. My adult spiritual journey has been about shedding [dogmatic] statements, about experiencing a raw faith in the process of living, and about understanding that there is a discoverable meaning to living, a purpose for my being.

You probably didn't grow up with the spiritual or religious freedom that Quinn and other men like him have found in their recovery. It's much more likely that your concept of a Higher Power was defined for you. As Joe H. said:

I was raised in the Catholic Church and went to Catholic school— there always was a sense of being watched and that you could be reprimanded at any moment. Recovery has allowed me to let go of those old beliefs about faith and start a relationship with God.

Your definition of God probably influenced the way you experienced your life and the world around you—which means that that definition also influenced how you saw yourself as a man and what you thought about other men and women. Ask yourself these questions:

- *How did others define your Higher Power for you?*
- *Did your Higher Power punish the wicked and reward the good?*
- *Was your Higher Power's love conditional?*
- *Was your Higher Power a male figure?*
- *How do you think your attitudes about being a man, about your relationships with others, and about your life, in general, were guided by your ideas about your Higher Power?*

I was in an abusive relationship with my Higher Power for most of my childhood and adolescence because I had confused my alcoholic, temperamental father and God. That relationship with God defined how I experienced the rest of my world! I had no idea that there were different and perhaps more helpful ways to think about God.

Defining your Higher Power may be confusing. You can decide what it is and is not. Dan J.'s comments can help you begin this process:

> When I got to AA, I had been beaten down by alcohol and decided to reinvent my God based on the suggestion in the [Big] Book to create my own understanding of him or her. I threw away all the things I was told as a child and started believing in something greater than me, even though I didn't know what that was. I still don't fully understand it. I just accept that there is a God and I am not it. When I can do that, I am in a much better place both mentally and spiritually.

The words *as you understood* open the gates to faith for many of us who never would have found it otherwise. You may not fully understand right now the incredible opportunity you are being given, but that's okay. Understanding will come with time and effort as you work Step Three. Your challenge is to let go of the ideas that get in the way of what is possible in your new relationship with your Higher Power.

Out of Control

For most men in Western culture, the quest for power, happiness, and even peace grows out of control. From an early age, we were taught to control ourselves and the world around us—our environment, other people, ourselves, and our emotions. Kerry talked about this, "I was always taught to be tough, independent, and always in control." He then went on to talk about how, because of his addiction, he had "obviously lost the 'in control' part of being a man."

As you watched older men such as your father, uncles, neighbors, or others in your life, you saw that they were powerful and often seemed to be in control. What you didn't know, however, was what was going on inside of those men. Now that you are an adult and know how often you have felt fear, anxiety, insecurity, sadness, and confusion—and that what you do and say doesn't always reflect how you actually feel—you might now realize that there was more going on in those men than you ever knew. Perhaps, much more. As Chris said, "I grew up with a father who tried to act like he was in control, but I knew he wasn't."

Do you believe that being a man means being in control and that control leads to success? Do you think you deserve to be in control just because you're a guy? Many men seek control primarily for one reason: because of the uncomfortable feelings—fear, insecurity, vulnerability, and doubt—that arise when they do not have control. To avoid those feelings, they try to control the people, places, and things in their life. Unfortunately, those attempts rarely work.

In the chapter on Step One, you read that if you want to take control of situations or relationships, sometimes you will be given that control just because you are a man. Control may work in the short term, or you may get what you think you want, but at what cost? Stop for a moment and think about the ways you've tried to control other people and events. What was the result? What you hoped? What relationships have you strained, or even lost, in your attempts to control them? What opportunities have you lost?

Chris talked about this:

There's a lot of turmoil that happens for anybody when you think you are in control of things. Especially with people. Especially when you try to control what somebody else is doing or thinking . . . So for me, the Third Step is really showing me that I don't have any control, and that's been shown to me over and over again.

Here's part of this Step's challenge: Do you feel comfortable and safe enough to surrender the illusion of control that's been causing you and others so much suffering? Are you willing to let go of the need to be in charge? Pursuing the illusion of control can become a full-time occupation when you believe that control offers safety and security. But it doesn't. Your attempts to control actually sabotage the natural flow of life, and that causes most of your pain. Are you willing to trust in this Third Step wisdom, even if you don't believe it? Or at least suspend your doubt?

Through Step Three you can learn to live surrendering to the reality of life and accepting that your perception of control is indeed an illusion. As Peter said:

It was the bursting of that myth that I had control. It is so limited with what I realistically do have control over. I cannot really even control my thinking, but I can choose to pursue a thought or not to pursue it.

Thoroughly and honestly practicing Step Three is fundamental to your ongoing recovery. When we don't, working the remaining Steps is like building a house on a weak foundation. Talk to any old-timer and he will tell you that he is constantly recommitting to work Step Three. Casey said it very well:

For me in early sobriety, the first working of Step Three was more along the lines of saying the Step Three prayer and moving on immediately to Steps Four and Five. I wasn't ready immediately to turn things over—it just didn't happen. But through the process of working Steps Four through Twelve, I finally started being comfortable with Step Three.

Nobody practices Step Three perfectly. And that's not the goal. Progress, not perfection, is the goal. You will fall back into your controlling behaviors at times. Maybe even often at first. But that's okay. Try to recognize what's happening, remember you have a choice, and then do something different—including going back to Step Three.

Of course, some degree of self-control is necessary. The struggle seems to be in finding a healthy discipline, of exercising the appropriate amount of control. If you've spent much of your life trying to control nearly everyone and everything—and deluding yourself by thinking that you actually were in control—how can you know what a healthy amount of control even looks like? There are no easy answers to that question. Through trial and error, and with the help of your sponsor and those in your meetings, you'll find a healthy balance in time. The foundation of long-term recovery includes self-discipline and appropriate control.

Willingness Is the Key

Step Three says you make a decision to turn your will and your life over to the care of your Higher Power. You are no longer in charge, and you do not get to have your way simply because you think you should. You were most likely not raised to approach your life this way. The constant pain of trying to live your life run only on self-will, however, is its own teacher. In Step Three you are saying, "Higher Power, I trust that your will is what is best for me." You recognize that living according to your will does not bring you happiness. Chris said:

> *I try my best to do the things I need to do no matter how hard . . . and know that I'm not in charge of everything . . . but my will is always there . . . I know God's will is a hell of a lot easier than mine. It shows me who I really am. I meet myself every time I do God's will.*

Yes, you will fall back into self-will and control at times, and especially early in your recovery, because you'll experience uncomfortable emotions and expect certain outcomes from life. We always want to take our will back. You must also realize that when you fall back into self-will and control, there are consequences for others. Your fear—your control and attempts to assert power over others—often hurts others and limits their freedom. You must look carefully at your behavior and be accountable for the effects your actions have on others—actions too often driven by unrestrained feelings. Look at yourself without judgment and let go of control. As Casey said, "To me progress in Step Three means a lot less of the control obsessions, managing the outcomes, and flying off the handle when something doesn't go my way."

As you read in Step One, being goal-oriented and having a fierce determination to get things done are two great qualities many men possess, and they offer you another way to look at the concept of willingness. When you set your mind to accomplish a goal, you want to make it happen. Step Three is not telling you to give up or to stop exercising this kind of resolve; you just need to align it with your Higher Power's will.

When you align your willpower with your Higher Power's will, you will have much more success and feel a greater sense of peace. The work of recovery is challenging. Your Higher Power will show you the way, but you have to walk the path.

The more you practice this Step and truly come to believe in a power greater than you, the more you realize that your will and your life are already in the hands of your Higher Power.

It's easy to become confused about Step Three. You may ask, "If I turn my will and life over to my Higher Power, what do I have to do?" This question will lead you to one of the great paradoxes of recovery: you turn your will over to your Higher Power but only your willingness and your willpower will make that effort meaningful. Willingness is when you use free choice to live your life. In Step Three, only your willingness can allow you to let go of your will and of your agenda for how life has to be. The *Twelve Steps and Twelve*

Traditions talks about this idea toward the end of the discussion of Step Three:

> But now it appears that there are certain things which only the individual can do. All by himself, and in the light of his own circumstances, he needs to develop the quality of willingness. When he acquires willingness, he is the only one who can make the decision to exert himself.[2]

You, alone, are responsible for developing willingness and taking the appropriate action. Your willingness is the key that opens the door to a faith that works, and your willingness becomes the foundation of your recovery. Do you have the willingness to not pick up a drug? To believe? To let go? To ask for help? To work the remaining Steps? To do anything to stay sober? Again and again and again? Only you have control over your willingness—over your life; only you can take the actions that will save your life. In Step Two you acknowledge you need help, and that it's okay to need and accept help. But knowing you need help is not the same as asking for that help.

Help!

Men in our culture are not known for our willingness to ask for help. As Casey said:

> Whether it's the male script or the alcoholic in general, or me specifically . . . I don't like people helping me. I have a tough time accepting help.

Men especially think asking for help means we are weak. Incompetent. Most of us grew up with fathers or other men who did not often ask for help or admit that they did not know what they were doing. The larger-than-life male characters in movies and on television mirrored this cultural lesson. They were strong, self-reliant, and unemotional. These men had all of the answers, and we never saw them ask for help—no matter how badly beaten they were.

Miguel talked very openly and honestly about the thoughts he struggles with when watching his teenage son:

If he needs an excessive amount of help with something that I feel he should just step up and do, I have to hold my tongue. I want to say, "Don't be a baby" or "Don't be a pussy" . . . Those thoughts are always in the back of my head because of how I grew up.

Fortunately, Miguel won't say those things to his son. He's aware now of the damage such words cause. Miguel also talked about the inner dialogue he had with himself about those same challenges. His struggles show how imbedded that teaching is in our lives as men.

There are many reasons why you might resist asking for help. Asking for help means that you have a problem and even worse, that you do not have the answer. You may think that if you talk to someone about your problems and admit how you are feeling, you'll be seen as weak or a failure. Casey went on to talk about how getting a sponsor "was terrifying because just the act in and of itself implies weakness and vulnerability. You are acknowledging you need help." When I asked him what that meant, he replied, "That you, in some respect, are a failure and you are weak." If you're at a point where you don't believe that anyone really cares about you, asking for help is frightening. What if the person says no?

That would only be more proof that you're worthless. Sadly, as a result, many of us in recovery do not ask for help until we have been beaten down by a problem, just as we've been by our addiction.

The ability to ask for help (and to keep asking) is a core part of practicing Step Three. It's absolutely vital to your ability to achieve long-term recovery and emotional sobriety. Steve, who is fifty-five years old with more than two years sobriety, said, "I realize today that it is a strength to realize you need help and be able to ask for it." Chris said it very well, too:

> It takes a lot more courage to ask for help than to suffer through something. I really do not care anymore what other people think of me for asking for help.

Some of us, in the depths of our despair and confusion in sobriety, finally reach out for help. Others pretend that everything is okay and keep their problems to themselves. The choice men make between the two approaches very often determines who stays sober and who does not. In life, the "strong and silent" types, the heroes of many of our movies, are more than likely to die from their addiction.

The Care of Your Higher Power

Practicing Step Three may bring up uncomfortable feelings of fear, insecurity, vulnerability, and doubt. You have to take the risk of believing that when you reach out to your Higher Power for help, when you let go, you will be okay. You are turning your will and your life over to the care of your Higher Power and the word *care* implies goodness and safety.

For those of us who have come to see the world as a hostile and unsafe place, Step Three offers a new way of experiencing it. Your Higher Power will not turn against you, abuse you, betray you, or hurt you. The belief in the inherent goodness of your Higher Power can become the foundation of your faith. Faith will help you to see that the world is a safe place. It provides the foundation to work the remaining Steps. As Charlie said:

Step Three changed my whole concept and relationship with God. I now feel a part of all life and love. I know that a power greater than me really does love and care for me.

Thy Will, Not Mine

A question every devoted Twelve Step member struggles with is this: what is the Higher Power's will? You can put yourself into a tailspin attempting to discover your Higher Power's will. In truth, knowing your Higher Power's will for you is not that difficult. Your primary role is to be open and to pay close attention—because your Higher Power's will can come to you in any number of ways. Your biggest job is to continue living your life by working the rest of the Steps one day at a time and trusting your group and sponsor to provide the Good Orderly Direction you need. The rest will take care of itself.

Living in the present moment makes it easier to discover your Higher Power's will. Your ability to focus on the present moment and on the activity in which you are engaged helps you tap into a power greater than self. One action at a time, your Higher Power's will can unfold into a tapestry of days that become weeks and then years—with a final product called your life.

Perhaps, in the end though, Abraham Lincoln said it best: "Nobody knows God's will. We simply have to do the best we can."[3]

Letting Go

Some of us approach Step Three intellectually, with the Steps becoming a kind of checklist. Step One? Check. Step Two? Got it. Step Three? Did that one, too. Many men see their lives as a checklist, too. Grow up. Go to school. Get a job. Get a wife or partner. Have kids. Check, check, check . . . and when things don't seem to be working out, we try to force the issue. Control things. Make everything fit the plan. When you are *really* working Step Three, you'll probably find that it's very difficult to let go. Unfortunately, you cannot let go of a problem, person, or idea just by thinking about it. You have to actually surrender, with your whole self—you have to experience letting go. Step Three throws down the gauntlet: if we are going to live the Twelve Steps, we are going to be living in a wholly different way.

Many years ago when my father was very sick from his alcoholism and I had just moved to Kansas, a woman in recovery named Jane showed me how to turn my concerns and worries about my father over to my Higher Power. She taught me how to let go. I spent a lot of time in fear of my father dying. That fear led me to be hurtful and critical toward my father, and I regretted that every time I hung up the phone. The fear kept me up at night and had me reacting every time the light blinked on my answering machine. Jane could see what the fear was doing to me and she told me:

Dan, I want you to go home. Get on your knees and open up your arms. I want you to give your father to your Higher Power and trust that he is going to be okay. That whatever happens—and I mean whatever, Dan, including your worst fear—you and he will be okay. I want you to pray for your father to find peace. I want you to let go of him. As hard as it may be—let go, Dan.

And I did. Every night and every morning for the next several weeks. Sometimes with clenched teeth. Sometimes with great fear. Sometimes with great peace. When the call came only a few weeks later telling me my father was dead, I knew that I was going to be okay. Through the pain of the grief, I did not think of drinking. While his death was far from the outcome I desired, I knew in my heart that my father was finally at peace.

One day while my friend Stephanie was talking about letting go, she showed me another way of thinking about this concept. When we think about letting go, it's easy to imagine someone hanging from a cliff by a branch and then letting go. Falling. "There is another way to let go," Stephanie said, grabbing a ball. She held the ball so tightly you could see the whitening of her knuckles. Then, she relaxed her grip, took her fingers off the ball, and opened up her palm with the ball resting in the center. "This is also letting go." It's easy to think that if you let go, you'll lose whatever you are holding on to so desperately. When you clutch fear, anger, or whatever you are holding so tightly, your hands become full and you're unable to hold any of the joy, love, and peacefulness that might be right there in front of you.

You believe in an illusion when you think that you actually have control. Most of the time, the pain of holding on is simply the pain of denying reality. My father's life was never in my hands. Though I tried desperately, I never had any control over him. The majority of the people, places, and things you try to control were never, and will never be, in your control, and continuing to try to control them will be futile, and only bring you more frustration and pain.

Freedom

When we're active in our addiction, we're quite predictable. We have little spontaneity and spirit, and almost no sense of awe. Life is nothing more than slow suicide. Every day at the same bar. Every day the same routine. Sleepwalking through life, we become caricatures of ourselves, living a life of quiet desperation. The blessing of recovery gives you the opportunity to break free from this prison and begin to live in the freedom of the spirit. You can begin to live in the moment, being as unpredictable as you need to be. Life comes full circle: when you turn your will and your life over to the care of your Higher Power, you finally have the freedom to be who you are. Reggie talked about Step Three this way:

The decision to turn my will and my life over to God as I understand Him is a tremendously powerful thing. Knowing that I have a relationship with my Higher Power that can inform me about life and living is almost like having an unfair advantage in all situations. Learning to see God's will in everything has become my way of facing the world and all it can throw my way.

When you practice Step Three on a daily basis, trust the wisdom and care of your Higher Power, and let go of your need for control and power, you will discover the true meaning of freedom.

STEP FOUR

Made a searching and fearless moral inventory
of ourselves.

This Step is the one that
changed everything.

– REGGIE –

You tell many stories about yourself. Who you are, who others think you are, who you have been, who you want to be. Together, these stories make up the tapestry of your life. Though you've created these stories, you've not necessarily checked to see if they're true. You also keep your stories to yourself, from yourself, and from others. Many men secretly believe that nobody wants to know their whole story, and if others did hear it, they would no longer be worthy of love. Step Four gives you the opportunity to look at your story in depth, focusing on three core areas of your life: resentments, fears, and sex. You can begin looking at yourself "warts and all." As the Big Book reads:

> . . . *We searched out the flaws in our make-up which caused our failure. Being convinced that self, manifested in various ways, was what had defeated us, we considered its common manifestations.*[1]

Your challenge is to be fearless, honest, thorough, and objective as you look at yourself and your life. It takes courage to do this, and you need an element of faith and trust that this will be a worthwhile exercise. What you are looking for, with help from Step Four, is the right dose of self in your life.

I once heard a recovery speaker refer to working Step Four as "cleaning up your house and taking out the trash." Can you imagine what your house would be like if you only took the trash out once? As Chris said:

> For me Step Four has always been a very powerful Step, and it's important that I try to do it once a year just to clean house . . . It's all about finding out what my part is in things . . . What did I do, what have I not done, etc.

The house that is my life has grown over the years. I've found rooms I didn't know I had. Whole floors had escaped my awareness. I found stuff that I forgot I had, stuff that should have been tossed in the trash years ago, and stuff I wasn't ready to toss . . . until now. When I was younger I defined cleaning house as dusting off some furniture, vacuuming, cleaning the bathroom, and sweeping the floor. Today, I do a much more thorough job, and I do it more often. The same is true for my inner or spiritual house.

The following sections will help you avoid some of the obstacles you may encounter as you begin your personal house cleaning.

Selfish and Self-Centeredness

Yes, we guys can be seriously self-centered. The stories range from the humorous to the tragic: from the man who buys his wife front-row tickets to the hockey game or a riding lawnmower for her birthday to the guy who cannot see his partner's problems through the fog of his own more serious problems. But are men selfish or self-centered by nature? Absolutely not.

Selfishness and self-centeredness can grow out of pain and isolation, out of disconnection from your inner self and your Higher Power. It's possible these behaviors grew out of the powerful conflicting messages you internalized very early about being a man: that you are more important than you are and that you are not worthy of being treated as a valued human being. They grew from how your caregivers treated you and from the fear that you allowed to control your behavior so often and for so long. Your selfishness and self-centeredness also come from your very humanness.

Shame, Shame, Shame

Shame is a very powerful mix of emotions that says there's something deeply wrong with you as a person. Some men hide their shame with arrogance and self-importance, others hide themselves while they passively act out their anger and self-hatred against others. Whether we hate ourselves, are deeply unhappy, or simply clueless about our effect on others, we let ourselves believe that we can live this way because we are men. Regardless of how many smiles we flash to the world, this kind of life serves no one and offers us no real happiness. No matter how we try to deal with our shame, we can't seem to quiet that little voice that tells us we are not good enough, don't measure up, and we're not real men. Shame prevents us from connecting with others.

Brandon talked about how he discovered the shame in his life:

I always felt I was worth less than everyone else. It wasn't until I was able to release these dark feelings that I realized how powerful, influential, and dangerous they could be if I let myself react to them.

Shame hides the secrets that fuel your addictions. To get out from under your shame, you must first learn how to recognize when you are reacting out of shame and then how to look more closely at the situation that triggered those feelings. As Dave said:

I avoided looking at shame for much of my recovery. I saw any discussion of shame as ignoring responsibility. AA emphasizes how you need to take responsibility for everything. And as a result, I had a tendency to take responsibility for stuff that was not mine! Now, I see that shame is an important feeling to pay attention to because it helps me be responsible for issues that truly are mine.

The Twelve Steps are an excellent antidote for shame, and the elimination of shame begins with Step Four.

Contrary to what you may believe or have heard, Step Four is not meant as an opportunity for you to see and put down on paper everything "wrong" with you. Often you will experience shame about items on your inventory that have plagued you for some time. You may not be feeling compassionate toward yourself when you are doing Step Four. Few of us learned how to practice compassion either for others or ourselves. However, working the Steps without compassion for yourself will easily turn into an exercise of self-abuse.

Creating your own ritual as you do this work can help you feel compassionate toward yourself. For example, some men meditate for a period of time and pray for guidance before they begin. You could approach your prayer by thanking your Higher Power for fearlessness and thoroughness in completing your inventory. You could even light a candle to create a sacred space. As you recognize the spirituality connected to this Step—or as you give this Step a greater feeling of spirituality—you will approach the task with more gentleness. Find the balance between being fearless and thorough in your self-examination while still holding in your heart the spirit of Step Three—having turned your will and life over to the *care* of your Higher Power.

On the other hand, be careful that you don't use compassion as an excuse to ease up on the thoroughness of your inventory. Be hard on yourself, as the Big Book instructs us. Let yourself experience the pain and do not cut any corners in the process of self-examination. You will survive the pain of this Step. You deserve to be free of it. But you must do the work; you must be fearless and thorough! Casey talked about his experience writing his Step Four inventory:

> There was a lot of pain in some of that stuff that I shared. And a lot of shame . . . It was not an easy process, but it was a powerful process. It required a lot of courage and a lot of work.

Drama Kings

While men often accuse women of being drama queens, that is, being overly emotional and exaggerating their life situations, men can be drama kings. Step Four is the time you begin to unravel the drama in your life: the judgments, the exaggerations, the selfishness—all of the external dressing you have put on the events in your life that have kept you from seeing the truth about yourself and your experiences.

The dramas, the stories you've told yourself for years, have convinced you that you are a victim. You wrote the drama so that no matter what you did, felt or thought, no matter what happened or what went wrong, it was someone else's fault. You let yourself off the hook so you could justify your actions. Dan J. described this well when he said, "Before I took responsibility for my actions, nothing was my fault or my problem; it was yours, and I could justify it about a hundred different ways." Constantly casting yourself as the victim gave you an excuse for not being responsible for your life. Now you are being asked to grow up and be responsible for your actions, and part of that means learning and admitting when you're playing the victim. Asking you to look at yourself in this way is not meant to be shaming or judging; rather it's meant to empower you and lead you to a life that is, as the Big Book says, "happy, joyous, and free."[2]

The Big Book tells you that you are in "a fact-finding and a fact-facing process."[3] Be objective and be honest. Keep to the facts. Challenge the thoughts. As you look back, pay attention to the assumptions you were making about situations and the people involved. What feelings were involved? Try to look at the resentments you have without judgment.

Without drama. Try to see the facts amid the resentments. That will help you begin to see your resentments and, most important, your part in them.

If you follow the guidelines in the Big Book and *Twelve Steps and Twelve Traditions,* the practice of writing an inventory can help you take a detailed look at each of the three problem areas. You will see that anger is not what you thought it was. You will see that fear plays a greater part in your life than you probably ever imagined. And, you will see that sex dominates more of your life than you realized and often keeps you from getting what you really want—love and happiness. Listen to Miguel:

Step Four was really the turning point in my life. I didn't have any understanding of who I was or where the drivers in my behavior were. I had no idea of the fears that I had; no idea of how selfish my behavior was. It was a really powerful Step for me.

Resentment and Anger

The easiest way
for me to respond to hurt is to return it,
and the vehicle to figure out how
to return it is anger.

– PETER –

The Big Book talks about creating a written inventory that includes your resentments. The Big Book gives you one of the most important tools for finding freedom from your anger, and it tells you that you are to put out of your mind the harms others have done you and resolutely look for your own mistakes.[4] The Big Book then tells you that, though the situation had not been entirely your fault, you must try "to disregard the other person involved entirely."[5] Chris said:

I realized that the resentment inventory on my list is a really big road block to happiness because when I resent somebody, it's my crap; it's my stuff. I need to realize that I need to get over it because typically it has nothing to do with what the other person has said or done.

This measure of personal accountability offers freedom. I have felt resentments vanish instantly when I have finally seen my part. For example, I once had a job at a treatment center. I had been so excited when I got the call letting me know the job was mine . . . until I heard the salary offer. It was much lower than I thought it should be. I did not have the courage to negotiate. I took the job and soon was full of resentment. While talking to Eric one night, I mentioned this resentment, and he helped strip it down to the facts. Then he said, "Who forced you to take the job?" As I finally saw clearly that I said yes to the salary offer and entered into a contract, I felt the resentment dissipate. Then, I laughed at myself. It was so clear. They had done nothing wrong at all!

Resentment Is Like Taking a Poison
And Expecting the Other Person to Get Sick

The Big Book states:

It is plain that a life which includes deep resentment leads only to futility and unhappiness. To the precise extent that we permit these, do we squander the hours that might have been worth while . . . For when harboring such feelings we shut ourselves off from the sunlight of the Spirit . . . If we were to live, we had to be free of anger. The grouch and the brainstorm were not for us. They may be the dubious luxury of normal men, but for alcoholics these things are poison.[6]

The essence of a resentment is the perception that you have somehow been harmed. In justifying your anger, you replay the incident in your head over and over, but ultimately, you suffer. You delude yourself by thinking that you are right and powerful. Have you ever noticed that while you are writhing from the emotional distress of a resentment, others are simply enjoying their lives? Think about this: why wouldn't you do anything to be rid of a resentment, knowing how much it hurts you? Your suffering does not serve you or others. I am constantly amazed at how many of us have internalized a need to suffer. Whether you think that your suffering somehow builds character or that you deserve it, you don't. A resentment is an act of self-abuse, period.

The solution for anger and resentment is the same as all Twelve Step solutions: a spiritual approach that includes gaining perspective on a problem before you act. Learn to identify and accept your resentments. Practice not acting on your anger. Learn to talk about your resentments and to see your part in them. What feelings are connected to your resentment? Were your feelings hurt? Did you feel slighted, embarrassed, taken for granted, or dismissed?

The Big Book also talks about praying for those we

resent. We can pray for the person to have a good (or great) life. Pray to better see others' suffering, or pray to see them as your Higher Power sees them. Let prayer replace the negative thoughts you have of others with positive thoughts. When you use prayer to counteract your resentments, you will begin to see that they are based in your decision to suffer. Eventually, you will see that your suffering is a choice.

Exorcising the Victim

Everyone feels at some point that they are, or have been, a victim. When we see ourselves as victims most or all of the time, however, we have a big problem. We all have the ability to play the victim, often with little or no awareness this is even happening. Many of us internalized our victimhood without realizing we had done so. Seeing yourself as a victim does not make you a bad person, and the point of this is not to judge anyone for feeling this way. However, playing the victim can prevent you from seeing yourself as you truly are and from growing as a person. You stay stuck in negative behaviors and stuck in your addiction.

Take a moment now and think about how often you feel and act like a victim. Be honest! Is it more than you realized? Unless you're willing to take a close look at yourself, you will not see the many ways that the victim shows up in your life.

Maybe you are focused on the abuse you suffered as a child, or on how you were treated because you were different in some way. Maybe you're thinking your coworkers and boss don't acknowledge your superior skills. It doesn't matter whether these situations are real or perceived; you will never find peace or serenity as long as you continue to see yourself as a victim. If you do not look closely, you won't be able to see the ways that the victim shows up in your life. You will need the help of others close to you, such as your sponsor, to help you see when you are acting like a victim. There is one clear signal that can help you spot when you are thinking like a victim: when you feel resentful toward some person, place, or thing. When you feel resentment, you've probably triggered your inner victim. Yes, there have been times when you truly have been victimized, but hanging on to the wrongs others have done to you does you no good. In fact, it gives them power and leaves you feeling angry, resentful, and powerless. So, you have a choice: you can allow that person to have that power over you or you can let go and forgive.

Of course, there are times when people experience horrible abuses and injustices. Some of us have experienced significant abuse and trauma, and we may not even realize the hold it has on our lives. As someone who has had to heal through his own abuse history, I can tell you that the people who helped me the most were the ones who told me that I was hurting myself by hanging on to the pain I'd been carrying from my past. They pointed out that how I was acting toward others was connected to events from my childhood—not because I was crazy or a bad person. They told me I was short-changing my own life today by seeing myself as a victim in the past. They helped me learn how to grieve the pain that

I had carried with me. They showed me that those experiences did not have to control my life, and that helped me to feel a sense of power and control in my life. They also challenged me to look at my behavior—regardless of how I felt. They helped me to see that my past did not have to define me; I did not have to repeat my father's mistakes. Today, I know that I have choices. You have choices, too. Learn how to let go of the victim and stop letting it run your life!

A Special Note: When you have any of those people who have been abusive to you in the past on your Fourth Step inventory, your sponsor and other men in the Twelve Step community will, with all good intentions, get you to look at your part. And you want to look at your part. For instance, I was a hyper kid with a loud and foul mouth who did not respect authority by the time I was eight years old. That was my part in how I ended up continuing to create negative relationships with those around me long into my adult years. But no matter what your part may have been and no matter what you may have done as a child or an adolescent, nothing makes the abuse you suffered acceptable or okay. Mike M. learned this about a physically abusive relationship he was in with another man:

> I hated myself for staying in the relationship, but I clung to this man for fear of never finding anyone better. In doing my Fourth Step work, I realized that there's never any "my part" when it comes to abuse. Working through this issue required a professional to help me get through it.

Know this: being abused was not your fault, it was not okay, and it was inexcusable. If that message is not also part of your Fourth and Fifth Step work from your sponsor and the men in the Twelve Step community, we have failed you.

For more on this topic, be sure to read the chapter titled "Men, Violence, and Trauma" beginning on page 231.

Underneath the Anger

One of the greatest lies about men, particularly in the Western world, is the story we tell about men's anger. The Big Book tells us that anger is "the dubious luxury of other people" and that for alcoholics anger can be deadly and put our sobriety at risk: "From it stem all forms of spiritual disease, for we have been not only mentally and physically ill, we have been spiritually sick."[7] Many of us walk around from relationship to relationship, day to day, pretending and thinking that we are angry. We are fooling ourselves and others into thinking that our biggest problem is anger. Anger, rage, and violence are far less than the sum of their parts.

Our culture is confused about men and anger, and so it is understandable that we men can also be confused. Some think that if we could learn to manage or control our anger, everything would be fine. Others think that men's anger and violence are a result of some inherent genetic disposition toward aggression.

Where *does* men's anger come from? Is it possible that something lies underneath the anger? Rich said, "I finally discovered that my anger, which I tried to control for years, usually masked other emotions, particularly fear—fear of losing something, not getting something, or having my comfort level affected."

I first learned that there was more to my anger than I ever guessed when one day early in my recovery, my counselor, Randy, confronted me:

Now hold on. You said that you cussed at your mother and threw the phone. You also said that you had been talking to her, and you thought she hadn't paid attention to what you were saying or didn't seem to care. That doesn't sound like anger to me. It sounds like your feelings were hurt, Dan.

In that moment, I was given back something that had been taken from me long ago—the right to be hurt. Then came the right to feel sad. The right to feel scared. These weren't new experiences, but I had buried them under many layers of anger and rage because I didn't want to look or feel weak. When I used drugs, I was able to dull the emotional intensity and numb the pain I felt, and when I stopped using, all the pain and emotion were waiting for me. I had hidden all of those feelings under the shell of the man I thought I needed to project to the world. I was tired of feeling powerless. Ninety percent of my anger was false or unwarranted. In reality, I was just begging for attention and love. Dan J. talked about his experience discovering the emotions that were driving much of his anger:

The only time I wasn't angry was when I was drunk or stoned. After I got sober, things didn't improve much. I was still holding in a lot of anger, and I couldn't keep it bottled up any longer. I still deal with anger now, but it has been much better since I discovered the two sources of my anger: fear and shame.

Too often, men don't know how to express anger. They turn it inward and suffer severe depression or isolation, or they use humor to hide how they are feeling. Others struggle to identify their resentments because they have stuffed their anger down so deeply. We men do not experience and express our anger in the same way, but we do have one common connection to our anger: the majority of us, particularly those of us who grew up in addicted family systems or who suffered abuse, do not learn how to appropriately express or even respect our emotions, especially our anger.

At some point in your life, you may have learned that anger, humor, or silence were the best ways to express yourself. Once learned, we carry that lesson for years. Your challenge now is to learn how to express your more vulnerable emotions in safe, respectful, and honest ways, and to find safe places to heal from your past trauma. Perhaps you are plagued by what another adult or older child did to you when you were younger. Maybe by what *you* did to someone. Or the fear of being hurt by someone who you have let into your heart because you have been hurt so many times in the past. No matter what may be driving the anger you feel, when you feel safe, have the support you need, and are willing to be honest about your behavior, you will be able to see what lies underneath your anger.

The Anger Funnel

Many men in our culture never learn how to name the feelings they are having. Without names for them, we have no way to tell one feeling from another. As a result, too many of us take the vast majority of our feelings—hurt, fear, insecurity, grief, sadness, depression—and place them in a funnel where they come out the other end as anger. Juan talked about the anger funnel:

If somebody hurt or rejected me—all of those emotions got funneled into anger because that's really the only emotion I knew. It was okay to feel anger. The anger—the masculine, the violent, the dominant, and the alpha—that was the place where those things were funneled because it was safe.

How does the anger funnel show up in your life?

Healthy Anger

Is anger ever justified? Are there appropriate times to be angry? Yes, anger can be a healthy emotion. When you see or experience injustice, you should feel angry. When you are unfairly treated or cheated, some level of anger is appropriate. As those you love suffer and die, you will feel angry at some point during the grieving process.

How you express your anger, however, is the key issue. How you behave when angry is much more important than how you feel. Venting to a friend or a sponsor, writing a letter, or simply feeling it are all healthy ways to express anger. Restraint is also a good option that can help to keep situations from becoming worse. When you practice restraint, you pause and think.

"Anger is okay. Anger is healthy," I remember my partner Nancy saying to me as she held my hands. The woman I had hurt with my anger was telling me, with nothing but love in her voice, that anger was okay. And because it was she who was saying this, I listened. This memory is of the first time I expressed anger at Nancy in a healthy way. I had sat with her in the living room and had calmly told her how I was feeling angry about some challenges in our relationship. A part of me couldn't believe that was really anger. That morning I had woken feeling the anger and then *while I was emotionally and spiritually centered,* I told her what was bothering me and that I felt some anger. I also told her I felt fear and hurt. I didn't yell, hit a wall, isolate, or blame her. I felt nervous talking to her. I told her, "This is hard for me. I want to yell right now." It took me a long time to get to that place and an even longer time to develop that into part of my regular practice that I use today.

As you explore healthy ways to express your anger, be careful. Some men in recovery and some professional counselors believe that hitting pillows or other objects, yelling, or role playing are effective ways to work through your anger. That may be true, but they can also feed the anger. Even worse, engaging in exercises like this can retraumatize a man without him having any idea that is happening (see the chapter titled "Men, Violence, and Trauma" on page 231). For the most part, such approaches may not be the best choice for you.

Another approach is to learn how to breathe through your anger, which is similar to the "count to ten before you do anything" method. This practice requires greater discipline and restraint.

Learn how to notice when you are getting angry, embrace your anger without judging yourself, and breathe into the feelings. Meditation can help you here as well (see Step Eleven).

Most of us feel shame when certain feelings arise. We start judging ourselves for having the feelings, and we may want to act out to get away from them. Juan talked about this:

If I'm feeling vulnerable about something, if I come at you and "attack" you, you won't see that I'm actually feeling vulnerable. My technique is to intimidate with my masculinity and power so you won't see that I am really a vulnerable person. That [behavior] is my shield.

Chemically dependent men know all too well the overpowering effect of emotions. When we feel safe and are given permission to be vulnerable, most of us will dip our feet into the water. At first you may not want to admit any feelings of fear, hurt, or shame. After a while, though, you'll begin to feel alive again—and free, relaxed, and comfortable in your own skin, perhaps for the first time in your life. When you tell other men and women that everything is going great, it'll be true. Many men say that once they realized it was safe enough to be vulnerable, honest, and open about their experiences, they felt immense freedom. You will, too, and you'll also discover, at last, the man underneath the anger.

A Special Note: If you are reading this section and you or others have had concerns about your anger being expressed as rage, abusiveness, or violence, *get help now*. While working Step Four will help you, you may still need additional help. When your anger turns abusive, it becomes a serious problem for you and others around you. When your anger turns into violent behavior, you are dealing with a serious problem. Pay close attention to your definition of *violence*. Chances are you will need to broaden it. Many of us assume that violence is physical hitting, but there are many behaviors that are violent—many that you may think are actually helping you to avoid being violent. It does not matter if deep down you are feeling afraid, hurt, or full of shame: *the violence must stop.* You need to be accountable for your actions so that people around you are safe. Unfortunately, a lot of people close to you may not know how to respond to your violent behavior. They need help and support too and you should encourage them to get that help. In his heart of hearts no man, especially those of us in recovery, wishes to hurt and harm others. You need to get help, heal, and stop the anger and the violence, or true recovery will always remain elusive. See also the chapter titled "Men, Violence, and Trauma" on page 231.

Fear

> *To me, these last two years have shown*
> *me how much fear there is in my life as*
> *a sober person who has eight years of*
> *recovery. I knew I was afraid, but I didn't*
> *know why or where it was coming from.*
>
> – CHRIS –

All men experience fear even though many of us resist admitting it. The gift of Step Four is not freedom from fear, but freedom from the stranglehold that fear can have over you. Chris, with eight years of sobriety, was preparing for Step Five. His sponsor told him to pay close attention to the fears section of the Step Four inventory. He challenged Chris to look at every fear he had and list it on his paper. He then challenged Chris to look at what fears might be underneath those fears and list them as well. As Chris was working on his inventory, he was amazed that he had so many fears. "Where the hell did these come from?" he asked his sponsor. "I have eight years of sobriety. I am not supposed to have these fears!"

The majority of us accepted this idea long ago, and it's probably become invisible to you now. And that is another one of the lies. We often tell ourselves that as men, we are not supposed to be afraid. Casey talked about how he discovered his fears several years into his sobriety:

If you go to good meetings, you will hear a lot of guys talking about fear. I've seen big, thick lumberjack types or high-powered lawyers talking about fear. At first I just couldn't grasp it. I told my sponsor I wasn't afraid of anything. It wasn't until much later in sobriety that my fears became very apparent, and I was really able to see that fear was underlying every one of my defects of character.

Casey learned not to admit his fears and to believe that he was not afraid of anything. Casey's attitude about fear is much different now:

You see all of these guys with those "No Fear" stickers. A friend of mine and I were joking about getting a sticker that said "Scared Shitless."

The belief that men shouldn't be afraid of anything runs deep in our culture. But it's simply not true that men don't have fears. Being afraid does not mean that you are weak or less of a man, that you are crazy, a "pussy," or a "baby," and so on. It simply means you are experiencing the natural emotion called *fear.* Dan J. talked about how fear affects his life:

Fear is my life. I am a fear-based person. I have been that way as long as I can remember. When faced with fear, I often run. I try to avoid it. It truly is the "evil and corroding thread" of my existence. Every day I try to be a little more comfortable in my fear and act with courage.

The more you are able to experience your fear without judgment, the better you'll be able to look at your fear honestly and with compassion.

The Big Book addresses fear in this way:

This short word somehow touches about every aspect of our lives. It was an evil and corroding thread; **the fabric of our existence was shot through with it** *[emphasis added].*[8]

Without drugs, fear and anxiety can become overwhelmingly present, which is one of the reasons fear is discussed so often in Step Four. Bill W. and the other first one hundred men and women clearly understood that fear was the underlying cause of much pain, which is why they said it should be classed with stealing because "it seems to cause more trouble."[9]

Twelve Steps and Twelve Traditions talks about how most of our fear is based on one of two perspectives: thinking we will not get something that we want, or that we will lose something that we already have. Your needs may seem bottomless because you see happiness as finite—only so much to go around. This can create strong feelings of insecurity, loneliness, and fear. When you are in constant competition with others, it's difficult to realize that there is enough love, peace, and security for everyone . . . including you.

Do not babysit your fears. Yes, you are experiencing fear. So what? How long are you going to use fear as an excuse to not live up to your values? Challenge yourself to always describe situations that are causing your suffering as honestly as you can. Look for layers of fear—very often underneath one fear is a deeper fear.

Peter talked about this idea:

That's what I'm terrified of, that no one is going to want to be around me. I'm going to be deserted and abandoned. Those two fears drive most all of my fears.

You will fully experience the freedom offered in recovery when you free yourself from your fears.

The best antidote for fear is a faith rooted in Steps Two and Three. Many of us believe that analyzing a situation is the best way to find the right solution or next step. That analysis leads us to believe that we have the answers. It puts pressure on us to figure things out. When we believe that we must have the answer or that we always have to be in control of the outcome to a situation, we invite fear into our lives. That is why we speak so often of faith being the opposite of fear. When I do my due diligence for any problem or situation that I am facing and am then able to trust that "all is well" and that I will be okay no matter what the outcome, I am living in faith. And fear has much less impact on my life.

The power of Step Three is that when you turn your will and life over to your Higher Power, you understand that you are going to be okay. How do you really know that everything is going to be okay? How do you know if you do not run from your pain that it will serve your recovery? Turning it over by definition means that you do not know this. You have to take it as a matter of faith.

The question you really need to ask is, how has your life been served by running from pain? How is that approach working for you? You have only two choices: to live in faith or in fear.

Men who act despite their fear we call brave and courageous. They accomplish incredible feats that are awe-inspiring. These men can cry in front of the people they care about. Stay in partnerships that ask a level of intimacy they have never known. Commit themselves to fatherhood for the love and care of their children. Create relationships with other men that are honest, deep, and vulnerable.

You can transcend your fear. You begin when you realize that you are simply experiencing fear. Perhaps one of the best ways to summarize our relation to fear comes from Joe P., who during twenty years of recovery has had the same mantra from day one: do it scared.

When I learned of my father's death, I felt the greatest punch from the universe I had ever felt. There was only one way I could get through it: Face Everything And Recover (FEAR). It starts with faith, with some belief that what the others in recovery are telling you is true. Then your own experience begins to show you that when you face your problems, when you get help and support, when you decide to grow up, and when you take responsibility for your life, one day at a time, you recover. As faith grows, fear lessens. Face Everything And Recover can become your mantra—a mantra you have the opportunity to live each day.

Sex

Now I realize that my sexuality has been a bigger motivator for me than I ever knew. I've only recently come to realize its power and influence on my behavior. It is sex that has overpowered my conscience and has been the dictator of my actions in many a situation.

- BRANDON -

Most men come into recovery with many challenges in the area of sex. It does not matter if we have never been in a committed relationship, been in a committed relationship once, or been in a committed relationship multiple times. It does not matter if we are straight, gay, bisexual, or just confused. Few of us have been thoughtful about how we want sex to fit into our lives. Many of us had our sex lives start under the influence and continue under the influence. As a result, when we first enter recovery, we have an overwhelming fear of being sexual with another person while sober. As Casey said, "I went from sleeping with anyone, from not caring at all about the act of sex, to being scared shitless about sex."

The Big Book talks about our sex lives as essential to

who we are as human beings. Having a healthy sense of sex and a positive sexual identity, which are essential to a successful recovery, are difficult for us. When you at last begin to honestly look at your adolescent and adult sex life, you begin to create a healthy sexual identity and experience.

Some of us resist being brutally honest and hide behind some degree of bravado about the sex inventory. Some take pride in saying they've slept with a large number of people. Homosexual experiences and relationships can complicate matters even more because such interactions are contradictory to stereotypical masculinity.

The sex section of the Step Four inventory is our opportunity to learn how to have mature and honest conversations about sex, and to take a comprehensive look at our sex life. Fearlessness and thoroughness in this part of the inventory will allow us "to shape a sane and sound ideal for our future sex life."[10]

What does it mean to be thorough on this part of Step Four? Chris said:

I originally thought the sex inventory was just that—all about sex. It is not just about who I slept with. It is about the women I have hurt, the guys I have hurt (if my actions caused harm or hurt feelings). What are my motives? Am I flirting with someone to get something from them? It is not just about sex—it is about intimacy and relationships and how I have used sex to get those.

If you are thorough, you'll see that sex never existed in a vacuum, as much as you may have wanted to believe it did. You'll see the consequences of being irresponsible with sex.

95

You will begin to see how sex fits into your ideas about love, relationships, and intimacy. Andy said:

I have moved through my shameful feelings about sex and am able to communicate openly about sex. I see sex as another way to communicate with my partner in a meaningful and creative way.

Many of Us Needed an Overhauling There

If you cannot talk about sex with your partner then you probably should not be having sex. Many of us grow up with immature ideas and are confused about sex—though our ideals may be more evolved, we find it difficult to stick to them when we are using. When we get sober it may be easier to act on our impulses and think that sex—instead of using—will make us feel okay. Casey talked about the experience of one of his sponsees:

There's that whole "I'm not feelin' that great, I want to go get laid and I'll feel better." I had a sponsee who had been sober for maybe a year, and he was home one night feeling alone and depressed. He called up one of these chat lines, and two women who were prostitutes came over. He ended up sleeping with them, relapsing, as well as catching an STD. It's a very dangerous thing when we slip into the lonely and depressed mind-set.

Like a lot of men, when I was first sober sex scared me. I had had a good amount of sex—mostly one-night stands—and had never had sex sober. Some men coming into recovery can say the same, only it has been ten, twenty, or even thirty years for them.

The Big Book says, "We remembered always that our sex powers were God-given and therefore good, neither to be used lightly or selfishly nor to be despised and loathed."[11]

That means the shame that many of us often have about our bodies, our sexuality, and the act of sex itself is mistaken and useless.

For many of us the shame is tied directly to our religious experience growing up. Quinn talked about this:

Integrating a healthy sense of my sexuality has been a life's work. It remains the aspect of my life most mangled by my early Catholicism. Although I have much to be pleased with in this work, it remains a struggle.

Through sex, you have the opportunity for a union with another human being and your Higher Power in one of the most deep and profound ways available to you. Reggie said:

Prior to recovery, sex was an objective—something to achieve. In recovery, sex is an expression of love and connection with my partner.

Casey talked about why sex scared him so much when he first got sober:

It implies that I care about somebody. I didn't date for about three years in sobriety, and it's only been recently when I've had a little more healthy attitude about sex in terms of that it's a healthy act . . . versus being scared shitless of it.

We want to love someone and for them to love us. We want to feel the acceptance and grace that come from receiving another's love but have a lot of questions about how sex fits into our lives. Some of the questions you might be asking yourself are: How am I supposed to have a relationship where sex is only one part of it? How do I navigate the confusion, the doubt, the fear, and the discomfort? How do I learn to share myself? Why does it seem more difficult to have sex when you care about someone? Can I really love someone? Do I even know what love is? Why are sex, love, and relationships so scary, confusing, and complicated? Can I be comfortable with sex while not under the influence?

When we are learning how to date in sobriety, we often have few tools and little to no spiritual muscle to experience intimacy. Dominique talked about this:

In early sobriety, relationships were a complete mystery. I had to learn to date at forty. No fun. And the end of my first real relationship sent me into a deep depression of several months. It took awhile to learn the difference between sex (which was scary) and love (which was an unknown).

A lot of us use sex to connect. We look for the "friends with benefits" or no-strings-attached sex. Sometimes we live on one-night stands. Other times, sex defines the relationship, and we do not know what we like about our partners otherwise. And our desire for a deep connection with another human being is left unfulfilled. Brian is very open about the challenges he faced in his sexuality when he first got sober:

Prior to becoming sober and early on in recovery, I would describe myself as sexually inhibited, inadequate, confused, repressed, inexperienced, and insecure . . . Sex seemed dirty or impure . . . At times I even questioned my sexual orientation, though I have never had sexual relationships with other men. At other times I have turned to unhealthy outlets, including pornography, as a means of sexual gratification, though those behaviors have caused me feelings of guilt and shame . . . I really like what I have learned in the program about trying to shape a safe and sound ideal for sexual expression, while not feeling unduly guilty if I slip up.

If you cannot be honest about the secrets you keep regarding sex, you will not have a healthy sex life, and that's why you have to be fearless and thorough with your sex inventory. Give yourself that gift—you deserve it!

Sex and Intimacy

"The most fulfilling sexual relationships involve a combination of emotional and physical intimacy, along with a sense of trust and honesty," said Brian, one of the men interviewed for this book. He has it exactly right. When we only focus on getting laid (the conquest) or orgasm, sex is a selfish and domineering act that brings neither greater intimacy nor deeper love. We do not honor ourselves, our partner, or the sexual union itself. When we don't allow ourselves to experience the fullness of sex, we actually give up our sexual power.

Having a healthy sense of our sexual power grows out of the realization that we can choose when, how, with whom, and why we have sex. We often do not think of ourselves as having this choice, but sex is not as fulfilling and can often leave us feeling confused if we have sex when we do not want to. Sex should not be about just meeting your physical or emotional needs. To be truly fulfilling, sexual relationships involve love, compassion, and caring. We want to feel close to our partner, both physically and emotionally. We don't have to think of it in "either/or" terms. Sometimes we just want our partner to lie by us, listen to us, or just hold us. The challenge is recognizing those moments and knowing and asking for what you need. If you attempt to only use sex to take care of yourself emotionally, you'll end up being disappointed.

Pornography

You cannot talk about sex and men without addressing the issue of pornography. Many of the men I interviewed talked openly about their difficult relationship with the use of pornography. Dan J. was brutally honest:

I use porn to fill a hole that is left in me when I feel abandoned by those I love. My partner travels several times a year, and it triggers an insecurity in me that starts the ball rolling. I usually feel very afraid right before she leaves, and then I start planning ways to avoid the feeling by shutting down. I am scared and don't know how to deal with it. If I am in a good place spiritually I can find the strength to reach out to another person, especially if I know he has the same issue.

Because pornography can interfere with healthy sexuality, it's very important for you to take an honest look at the role pornography plays in your life. When you're feeling lonely and unloved, do you regularly turn to porn to make you feel better about yourself, at least temporarily? Turning to porn will not help you address whatever is getting in the way of a healthy relationship. If anything, the problem will worsen. Relationships are about negotiation and compromise. Talk with your partner. Does she or he know about your frustrations and concerns? Do you understand your partner's concerns? Talk about your relationship, what's working and what isn't, and get help if needed.

Pornography isn't necessarily unhealthy. Some couples use pornography to enhance their relationship. This more nuanced aspect of pornography is a challenge. I cannot tell you how or if pornography fits into your relationship or sex life. This is a very personal exploration. The first sign that you have an unhealthy relationship with porn is when your use becomes a secret that you keep from others, especially your partner. What is most important is that you are willing to look at how you use pornography, and to be honest with yourself, your partner, and any others from whom you've asked for advice about this issue. One thing to remember, though: many of the women (and men) in porn magazines and Web sites are being exploited, and by patronizing these venues, it can be said that you're playing a role in their exploitation. That might account for some of the healthy guilt many of us feel when we use porn for sexual gratification.

Sex Objects

A meaningful sexual inventory in Step Four must include looking at the issue of objectification. Too often men see or treat women (or other men) as sex objects rather than as a person. We are bombarded daily with images that objectify people, especially women, as sex objects. Gay or straight, these images are everywhere, and ignoring them and the messages they give is difficult. Men also can objectify women we don't find sexually attractive by simply ignoring them. How you view women (or other gay men) is also connected to your attitudes about masculinity, love, power, intimacy, and other aspects of your life. In the context of Step Four, it's very important to examine all the ideas and attitudes you have about people as sex objects, how you have treated them in the past, and any harm you may have caused. Juan said, "All of the women I had used sexually showed up in my sexual inventory."

Sexual Abuse

Many men in recovery are survivors of sexual abuse. While our society most often addresses sexual abuse of women, statistics clearly show that sexual abuse is a significant issue for a high percentage of men, too. Memories of past sexual abuse haunt many men, sometimes even driving them to commit such acts, too, particularly when active in their addictions and acting out their own trauma. Historically we have done a poor job as a society in talking about sexual abuse among boys and men. The pedophilia scandal in the Catholic Church in this country has finally brought this issue out in the open. Many men feel much shame about these experiences and have kept them even from themselves. These men often find themselves unable to be in or sustain any meaningful relationship. We must support our fellow men and help them find ways to identify this issue in order to learn how to talk about the abuse. When this issue arises during a Fourth Step inventory, sponsors and friends can best support this person by helping him get professional help to deal with the trauma in a healthy and effective way.

It's very important at this time to take an honest and thorough look at your sex life and at your whole sexual landscape. Don't let your fear of talking about sex prevent you from looking at your sexuality and defining your own experience of sex in a way that affirms your best self and your ideals. Let nothing be off the table with your sponsor, your therapist, your spiritual confidant, and especially your partner. You cannot help but open and enhance your spiritual life when you grow as a sexual being. When you learn to love your body and yourself and to see your sexuality as an integral part of who you are, you have a greater sense of the infinite and a much greater sense of peace.

STEP FIVE

Admitted to God, to ourselves, and to another human being the exact nature of our wrongs.

Admitting something that is dark, secretive, and humiliating is not something men seek to do under most circumstances.

- REGGIE -

In Step Five, you discover that sharing the story of who you are and who you have been is essential to your continued growth in recovery. First, though, you have to break one of the sacred rules of masculinity: never show weakness. Dave said:

In my mind, men were to be individually motivated, quiet, and unapologetic. The need for disclosure to save my life and establish a substantive relationship with God threatened this view of myself as a man.

In Step Four you were putting your heart and soul on paper but it was private. Now, Step Five asks you to share your weaknesses and vulnerabilities with your Higher Power and another human being. Rob said:

Admit my weaknesses to another man? Yes! And it will make me stronger.

Recovery transforms us, giving us more ability to share ourselves in our relationships. The beginning of that transformation is rooted in Step Five.

The Big Book states that the primary reason for Step Five is quite simple: "If we skip this vital step, we may not overcome [our addiction]."[1] That statement, alone, is reason enough for any man to do this Step. But look at the wording of the Step. You see the word *admit* for the second time. As we discussed in Step One, when you "admit" in the context of the Twelve Steps you are making an acknowledgment, a confession of sorts. In the confessional culture we live in, you need to understand and distinguish between real versus ego-driven self-disclosure. "Admitting the exact nature of your wrongs" is neither confession based on discovery of guilt (being caught with your hand in the cookie jar) nor confession based on a need for attention. In Step Five you free yourself of the burdens you carry—that which weighs you down as you walk through the world each day.

The confession of Step Five is based on the belief that when you reveal yourself *completely* to another person, something profound happens to you as a result. When you confess your resentments, fears, and sex inventory, this may be the first time that you share some of the most painful, embarrassing, and difficult events, times, and mistakes of your life. Many of us underestimate the vulnerability of this Step. Reggie talked about this:

Facing embarrassing things about yourself is cleansing and an enormously powerful experience. Coming clean with my sponsor, my family, and, most of all, myself were experiences that began to set me free from my past in a way I had never imagined.

In Step Five, we are admitting some incredibly personal truths about who we have been and who we think we are. We have violated our values and many of society's values. Some of us have committed harmful offenses. However, everything we have ever done is in the past. The idea that we do not have to define ourselves by what we have done and who we have been is what offers every man hope for a new life, a new story.

The story of our lives is often not what we thought it was. Men, and especially those of us with addictions, have often not been socialized or expected to practice much self-reflection, and we have developed few of the tools needed to do this effectively. We may be quite sophisticated in analyzing the behaviors and intentions of others, but the ability to turn that sharp gaze upon ourselves often proves limited.

In admitting our truth, we bring to light the story of who we are, and we ask another human being to help us reinterpret the story, to help us see the parts of the story we cannot see. To share your deepest darkest secrets with another human being and have him or her respond with acceptance and love is an amazing experience that every man should know. Casey spoke about this when he said, "Probably one of the most powerful things a person can do, I think, is to share completely all the good and bad with another person."

In Step Five we move out of isolation and into community, with help from our Higher Power and other human beings. Many of us were raised to be strong and silent, or at the very least to keep our problems to ourselves. Step Five offers entry into a whole new world. A world where we can be honest about our lives—our indiscretions, mistakes, struggles and successes—and not have to worry about whether we are measuring up or are good enough. A world in which people care about us and about what we have to say. A world in which people won't judge or abuse us for disclosing ourselves. Brian said:

> Women are stereotypically more likely to talk about themselves and to self-disclose, whereas men are more stoic and feel they should keep personal information to themselves. The process of sharing has allowed me to open myself up to others and to be viewed as a safe person to whom others can disclose and open up.

Community begins when we see that we are lovable and not so different from one another after all. Again, here's Casey: "It's just great because we realize we are all so similar; we all share the same stuff but it's just different names."

Love is what can happen in a successful Fifth Step. You might resist calling it love, but it is. As Charlie said, "Sharing my inventory was both an unburdening and the ultimate experience of being unconditionally loved." In the Twelve Step community, Step Five is when a man really begins to experience that he is lovable; from this point on we begin to truly learn to love ourselves. Dominique, a gay man who had been a priest for many years, had never talked about being gay or many of the behaviors about which he felt ashamed. Then he formed a bond with a female chaplain who gave him love and acceptance, which ultimately allowed him to accept himself:

She asked me if I really believed that I was the first gay priest she had ever met. She also told me that it was unlikely that we would be talking about anything that she hadn't heard before. Her powerful words encouraged me to open up.

Admitted to Our Higher Power

In Step Four, you admitted a lot to yourself, but you may or may not have been consciously admitting it to your Higher Power. When you invite your Higher Power to be present during Step Five and acknowledge the sacred aspect of this Step, you open yourself to greater intimacy. However, many of us have shame in our relationship with our Higher Power. We may have felt judged for our past, and as a result, it's difficult for us to believe that we can be forgiven. Consider starting Step Five with some meditation and prayer during which you invite the Higher Power into the process. Doing so will help you to know that your Higher Power is with you, and that you are not alone.

Admitted to Ourselves

Step Four was probably one of the first times that you really looked at yourself and your past. In Step Five, you have the opportunity to further admit to yourself everything you wrote in your inventory. Your life experiences will become more real as you hear yourself describing them to another person. Just as the burden of the problems and chaos that live inside your head lessens when you write it all down on paper, something equally profound happens when you share those problems and chaos with someone else. When you tell your story to someone else, you admit to yourself at a whole new level.

There's another reason for admitting to yourself in Step Five: *you* have to be a major party involved in this effort. *You* have to reinforce the existence of a new team—your Higher Power, you, and others. As you will often hear in the weeks and months ahead, your sobriety depends on your ability to cultivate a relationship with yourself. Some men review their inventory while looking at themselves in the mirror to reinforce the importance of literally admitting to themselves. Consider doing this, too.

Admitted to Another Human Being

You might be asking yourself right now why another human being is so necessary in Step Five. You might ask, "Why can't I just write everything down and learn from it? Why can't I just focus on a personal relationship between me and my Higher Power? Isn't that actually more intimate?" No, it's not because you will not reap the full benefits of this spiritual exercise without including another person.

In the discussion of Step Five, *Alcoholics Anonymous* states: "We think we have done well enough admitting these things to ourselves. There is doubt about that. In actual practice, we usually find a solitary self-appraisal insufficient."[2]

We all need to be very skeptical about our ability to effectively observe and analyze ourselves. A popular saying in the Twelve Step community tells us, "If you are sponsoring yourself, you are being sponsored by an idiot." This language is strong for a reason: we must interrupt the tendency we have to isolate ourselves and to try to solve everything on our own.

Many of the men interviewed for this book talked about how they never relied on anyone else to help them before recovery. They did not share their struggles and that of which they were ashamed because they did not have confidence that what they shared would not be used against them or kept confidential. As Vang said, "Step Five forced me to actually trust another man."

Most of us have many secrets that we've been keeping from those close to us, but the most dangerous secrets are those that we keep from ourselves. One of the greatest lies that addicts harbor is: "If you knew me—all of me—you would not love me. I am unlovable." When you keep the worst (or the best!) parts of you to yourself and sit as judge and jury over your own value, you become increasingly convinced that you're unlovable. Maybe you grew up in an environment in which punishment discouraged you from being honest about the mistakes you made. You probably grew up internalizing the message that said, "You *are* your mistakes"—and that kind of parenting is very shaming. And even today, that shame tells you to keep quiet about any of your mistakes or that which you find difficult to accept.

Shame lives in your secrets, and your secrets keep you sick. Step Five is about ending the secrets in your life.

In my twelfth year of sobriety, I discovered exactly how powerful one's secrets—and love—can be. I had been keeping a secret from myself and others for a long time. Shame had kept the door shut. Though I had told the men I sponsor many times that thoughts are only thoughts and they do not reflect who you are, I had been sitting with a demon that was haunting every interaction I had with my wife. This had gone on for the first four years of our marriage. During this time, she had been telling me how I was pushing her away to prove that I was unlovable. I could not see that at all. I just stayed stuck, acting out the drama with no awareness of the real problem. This secret was at the core of the anger that almost destroyed our marriage. Finally, I shared the secret with my counselor. Then, my sponsor. Then, one day, after a pretty bad fight, in tears, I shared my secret with my wife. To have her love me, to hold me while I cried in my vulnerability and fear, and to stay with me was a turning point in our marriage and for me in my own life. Never had I seen or felt so clearly the truth that our secrets *do* keep us sick *and* that the truth will set us free. Love is the only antidote I know for shame.

A Spiritual Experience: Into Me You See

More than anything, Step Five is about intimacy. Yes, Step Five addresses honesty, trust, and relationships, too, but these three experiences require intimacy—a genuine connection between two people.

Mentioning the word *intimacy* to men, though, can often be a great way to stop a conversation cold. As men, we are raised to see intimacy as the domain of women or we confuse it with sex. Mike M. talked about how Step Five changed his definition of intimacy:

> *I asked this new man to be my sponsor and explained to him that I had never had an intimate relationship with another gay man that wasn't sexual. Up until that point I had always inappropriately mistaken the word* intimate *to mean something physical.*

We discussed in the chapter on feelings how, for straight men, women are supposed to be the ones who deal with emotions in relationships, not us. They are supposed to create intimacy, and we are supposed to make fun of them for wanting it. We are raised to see intimacy as discussing sports scores with our friends. Or talking about cars, the news, girls, or telling jokes.

In Step Five, intimacy operates on three levels: with your Higher Power, with yourself, and with another human being. "Into me you see." As Peter explained, "If someone had told me five years ago that one of the most important parts of my life would be the intimate relationships I had with other men, those would've been fightin' words." Today Peter goes out of his way to come across the room to hug men and tell them that he loves them.

At this point in your recovery, you're probably feeling a growing expectation to be more intimate in your relationships. This is a positive change! Despite receiving little help from family or society with learning how to be intimate, we all want more closeness in our relationships. The catch is that most of us aren't sure how to get there. We may not have the words to ask for more from our relationships. Or we might not know how to respond when we're asked to be more intimate.

Chances are you didn't see conversations between your parents in which you could sense them being vulnerable with one another—talking about their relationship or some other aspect of their life—if such conversations even happened at all. If you didn't see intimacy in your parents' relationship, it's likely that you are afraid of intimacy or are unsure about how to be intimate. Yet deep inside, you want intimacy as much as any other human being.

By the time we are in a serious relationship, however, many of us are so emotionally shut down and our internal lives are so foreign to us that we resist anything that comes close to intimacy. Jo talked about this tendency to shut down at length:

My immediate response is always to shut down and walk away or escape. I think when I was a really tiny kid, I learned to run . . . I was crying and I was feeling bad and I learned that whatever I was feeling and how I was expressing it was wrong. So I stuffed that . . . You learn to run from your emotions . . . Then, as you grow a little older, you learn to run physically to get away from people . . . Eventually you learn how to run chemically . . . It's taken quite a long time for me to understand that when I want to get away, shut down, or run away, that's a part of my disease.

It's completely understandable that you haven't realized what you have been doing. One part of you may be asking for intimacy, while another part may be using insults, criticism, sarcasm, silence, and rage to keep intimacy as far away as possible.

In the Twelve Step community, you will learn fairly quickly that you are going to need to live your life differently if you want to stay sober and achieve lasting recovery. You will need to go to meetings and speak openly and honestly about what is going on in your life, and that's being intimate. Opening up to others. Being honest. Sharing. This can begin with your Fifth Step, and in time, intimacy will become one of the core vehicles to maintaining and growing in your recovery. Letting yourself become closer to others can bring rewards to you and your relationships that you cannot even imagine.

You probably didn't start recovery because you wanted to be a better man, partner, lover, father, brother, or son. You started recovery because your life had been sufficiently shaken up, and you were scared of dying or living a seemingly endless and miserable drug-addicted life. Or you were trying to save your relationship or your job, stay out of jail, or keep your kids.

Once you have stabilized your recovery, the process of spiritual growth will help you learn to be a better person, and thus a better partner, lover, father, brother, and son. What is amazing is that you can and will learn intimacy from other men in the Twelve Step community. That statement alone speaks to how different the world is for men in the Twelve Step culture. In that world we discover that we cannot just change the way that men think; we have to change the way we think about men.

STEP SIX

*Were entirely ready to have God remove
all these defects of character.*

**By becoming willing to have some
entity other than myself remove the
defects of character . . . I realized that I
didn't own the defects, that they weren't
the essence of me any more than my
thoughts or feelings were.**

– KIT –

You will hear old-timers say that Step Six is the one that separates the men from the boys. When we practice this Step on a regular basis we begin to grow up, no longer focused solely on ourselves and our every need. We begin to see that our true hope for a new life lies in letting go of our childish ways and embracing a new self-concept—one in which we walk through this world as men. As Dan J. said:

One thing I noticed early in my sobriety was that the guys were very immature. No one told us how to be a man, per se. It was explained that working the Steps would allow you to grow up and (hopefully) become more mature.

The "boys" are the ones who, with and without children, react to life with no awareness of the feelings and thoughts driving their behavior. They are living according to the dictates of our old friend, "Self-will run riot." Me, me, me.

Being the provider is not enough for men anymore; like it or not, society has changed its rules and expectations of us. We need to take responsibility for our emotional lives and realize that as men we are no better (or worse) than anyone else. Just because we are men does not mean we are endowed with some special right to exert control over others or get whatever we want. If you want to be a man and live in relationship with others, you need to assume your responsibilities as an adult, and Step Six will help you do just that. This process "involves the willingness and maturity to grow and develop character," said Brian.

Now that you've arrived at Step Six, you have uncovered some painful truths about who you are thanks to Steps Four and Five and your sponsor. You've begun to see the defects of character in the patterns of your behavior. And now, Step Six is telling you that you're ready to have God remove these defects of character. The Step also clearly states that you cannot remove the defects, at least not by yourself, and that idea contradicts what we men learn in our culture.

Almost without thinking about it, we men tend to look at most every situation in our lives and ask how we might be able to improve it. Most of us grew up with an unrealistic expectation that we can, and even need to, fix everything or solve every problem! We further assume that we know what needs to be fixed and how to fix it. This mentality might work well when it comes to home improvement and car repairs, but it has worked horribly when we applied it to people and our relationships. At some level, many of us believe that what we cannot fix, we cannot control . . . and what we cannot control can hurt us. While many of us have this conversation in our heads (although some of us may not be aware of it), we are not likely to admit it to ourselves or to anyone else. Think about this for a moment. Can you see that trying to fix everything by yourself contradicts the new relationship with your Higher Power that you made a commitment to in Step Three? Casey talked about this new relationship when he said, "I've gone from trying to be completely self-sufficient and capable of solving everything in the universe to a spot where I realize the benefit of sharing things with other people and looking for feedback."

A Defect Does Not Mean You're Defective

The concept of *defects* is often misinterpreted in the Twelve Step community. Here is one way to understand the concept. We all have defects of character, which you can think of as parts of yourself that you could improve. It's easy, especially for men, to confuse the concept of a defect with that of actually being defective. Defects merely prevent something from working as well as it should. Let's say that your car has begun to run roughly, and you have identified its defect as needing a tune-up. Does that mean it's shot and you need to junk it? Hardly! It just needs a tune-up and it will run smoothly again. Of course, we're a lot more complicated than a car.

In Step Six, you can use your Fourth Step inventory and the insights gained in doing your Fifth Step to identify your defects of character. It's an incredible opportunity to change how you live so that your life is more in line with your personal values and principles. You are the car; your Higher Power is the mechanic!

Step Six says we have ways of thinking and living that keep us from being our best selves. Our society today is obsessed with low self-esteem and constantly looking for anything that could potentially harm our fragile egos. As a result, the concept of defects of character is often misinterpreted to be overly negative and critical, implying that you aren't a worthwhile person if you have defects. The issue is not whether you are or are not worthwhile; you simply are a human being just like everyone else with your own set of worries, problems, and defects of character.

Your task now is to look at yourself: How are you living? What patterns of behavior are still getting in your way? What secrets are you still keeping? What would you change about yourself if you could?

When we change our behavior, our sense of who we are as men also changes. As addicts, we're used to our feelings dominating our lives and controlling our actions, and for this reason, we try to fool ourselves into thinking that talking in meetings about the men we want to be will suffice. Not so. As Rich said, "The best way to get self-esteem is to do estimable things."

Entirely Ready

The emotional and spiritual pain of recovery stem from letting your defects define what you think you know to be true about who you are, and from all the ways that you attempt to preserve that truth by hiding and protecting yourself and your ego. Those in the recovery community will talk about how, at some point in your sobriety, you will "run into yourself." By this they mean that eventually you realize that the majority of the problems you are experiencing can be traced to . . . you. The good news is that this gives you all the knowledge you need to become entirely ready to release to your Higher Power the defects that have caused these problems. Experience will show you that until you surrender to—meaning face and accept—whatever is troubling or challenging you, you will be in pain. What you resist will persist! Ultimately, in the depths of this pain, having prepared the way with Steps Four and Five, you become entirely ready.

Shame

To realize the power of Steps Six and Seven fully, you have another challenge to face: shame. Shame is not an emotion men like to admit to having. Yet all of us are haunted by shame about at least one aspect of who we are or about some part of our lives. Step Four helped you begin to address the impact that shame has had on your life. But after so many years of keeping those negative messages inside you, you are now beginning to see how deeply rooted shame is.

Step Five offered you a safe space to talk honestly about everything. Step Six offers you, probably for the first time, a safe and supportive place to learn, trust, and, most important, practice a whole new way of living. This will not be easy. Dave talked about the fear he feels every time he talks about something he's ashamed of:

> I constantly have to get through the fear of disclosing my mistakes and my thinking to other men whom I respect. Intellectually, I understand my friendships are not at risk, but still, each disclosure is full of fear. And at the same time, I always experience acceptance afterward.

What is working for Dave will work for you, too. Like Joe P. said earlier, "Do it scared!"

You have to actively work to release the stranglehold that shame has on your life, day by day. Think now about all those behaviors that you continue to engage in that you are too embarrassed to talk about in a meeting or with your sponsor. Those behaviors are exactly what you need to talk about now. This is how we demonstrate being entirely ready—by allowing people we trust to see the things about ourselves that shame has kept hidden. You must ignore the huge lie that shame tells you: that you are unique and alone. There are literally millions of others like you in the recovery community.

Shame also appears in all of the behaviors you still engage in that you are not embarrassed about but really should be. Your fellow men in recovery can help you to see that which you cannot yet see. The best support a man can give you in your recovery is to lovingly "smack you in the face" with his unflinching honesty in his commitment to support you in your emotional sobriety. As Steps Six and Seven grow more and more into the foundation of your life, you will find yourself able to talk about common behaviors and thought patterns that you've been keeping secret from others.

Laying Down Your Arms

Like Steps One and Three, Steps Six and Seven also require surrender. In Step One you surrender to your addiction; in Step Three you surrender the outcomes of your life to your Higher Power; and in Steps Six and Seven, you surrender to your humanity. Again and again and again. Humility is what makes surrender possible, and the practice of humility is essential to working Steps Six and Seven. "Getting ready to have God 'remove' my character defects," Reggie said, "was another way in which my powerlessness became obvious."

Choosing to surrender brings you back to the original struggle that kept you from getting sober—continuing to try in the face of repeated failure to control your use of alcohol and other drugs. Achieving greater humility and fully accepting your defects will likely be difficult because the concept of surrender, as we have discussed, is not a part of Western masculinity. You may acknowledge that surrender to your powerlessness over your addiction has brought you to this period of your sobriety. But surrender as a regular part of your life? How can that be effective? You may be thinking, "but to surrender is to lose, isn't it? Isn't losing only an incentive to try harder to win, to seek greater control, or to somehow regain the initiative to prove that I'm powerful, to prove that I am a man?"

Remember that one of the great paradoxes of sobriety is that in surrender, you find victory. You find freedom.

This pain, shame, and surrender are precisely why you need a loving and caring Higher Power in your life. If you feel as if you are alone in your pain and your shame, remember what you've learned in working the first five Steps: that your Higher Power is always there with you and for you.

A Lifetime Job

As I mentioned previously, many men come into sobriety seeing treatment and the Twelve Steps as a checklist. Go to treatment, work the Steps, and talk to your sponsor. Get better. Feel better. Done. Next.

It makes sense that men would take this approach: follow directions (like doing that car tune-up) and, *voilá,* problem solved. The blueprint for recovery offered through the Twelve Steps is not a repair manual. Rather, it's a design for living that is an ongoing and constantly unfolding process. The Twelve Steps are not a recipe for one dish; instead they teach you how to cook so you can create the meal you want! Work with them and you can create the life you want.

Step Six also reminds us that recovery is a lifelong job. You'll always find areas of your life in which you can make improvements. And you'll find that after a few years of recovery, you'll know much more about recovery and about yourself than you do now. Much of what I spent my eighth and tenth years looking at I had no real awareness of in my first, second, or even fifth year of sobriety. I was not yet ready or able to look at certain parts of myself. The same is true for you today: you don't know what you don't know either.

Andy, who has more than twenty years in Al-Anon, said that he sees Step Six as:

> *. . . adopting an attitude of change—and a change in attitude—about what it means to be a man. Many of my defects of character were caused by the conflict between who I was and how I thought I was supposed to be as a man.*

Andy is referring to those scripts we looked at earlier. Each of your character traits is part of the total script you follow. Step Six offers you the opportunity to look at each one and then determine if it represents who you really are or wish to be. Regardless of how men are supposed to be, you have the power to decide what kind of man you want to be.

By introducing you to your humanness, Step Six can help you to accept that you'll always find some area of your life in which you can grow. In recognizing your imperfection, and in solidarity with your fellow humans, you can also recognize your perfection in the eyes of your Higher Power. While the first five Steps may help you secure sobriety, serenity seems to come through the remaining Steps, beginning with Steps Six and Seven.

STEP SEVEN

Humbly asked Him to remove our shortcomings.

I definitely have the alpha male
"do it and get it done without help
from anyone else" mentality.

– KERRY –

Step Seven, like Step Six, will also help lead you to emotional maturity and to move away from the childish sense of entitlement we have discussed throughout the book. Those two areas of your life—emotional maturity and entitlement—are, in fact, quite connected.

Many of us men get sober but remain little boys in terms of our attitudes and actions. Emotionally we are, as another man in recovery dubbed us, "King Baby," an adult who still feels he has to get his way at all costs and no matter whom he harms. King Baby is the ultimate embodiment of men's distorted entitlement. Reacting to our emotions and driven by our self-centered neediness and fear, we think primarily of ourselves and what we want, and we expect others to bend over backward to provide it to us. We are often oblivious to how our actions affect others and what they need. As King Baby, we reign supreme in the desert of our own kingdom. Many times we get away with living in this bubble of entitlement because we are men. Either we have men in our lives who act like a wall for our behavior, providing strict boundaries and merciless feedback that help us grow up, or we go on living this way long into our recovery. We live out of our wounds, afraid to go deeper with the Steps. We find ourselves wondering why it seems so challenging to maintain relationships and to feel comfortable in our skin. We have a great deal of difficulty trying to live in a community that values love, tolerance, honesty, and respect because we feel great tension when our old beliefs and behaviors contradict those principles. Rich said:

I have returned to the values I learned and believed in as a boy and younger adult. More accurately, my behaviors are changing to more closely reflect my value system. The challenge for me is seeking help in comporting my behaviors to my moral values.

We struggle to successfully live in the world, to be *a part of it* rather than *apart from it.* Alcohol and other drugs once propped us up. They were the glue holding us together. Now that they're gone, we are forced to face ourselves completely and honestly. We must do this, or we risk relapse and death. Quinn explained it this way:

The experience of having a mirror held up to my face, of being confronted lovingly, has been a revelation. I have felt supported as an imperfect man. AA has been a safe place to examine my imperfections and focus on progress. The central experience of

*our mutual failure, and of our acceptance of one another for who
we actually are, has been the primary agent.*

The discipline of examining our defects of character and
humbly asking God to remove them is never ending. We are
never done with this Step, nor should we be. We confront
the fact in Steps Four through Six that we'll never be perfect,
but Step Seven will help us become the men we wish to be.

Character-Building over Comfort

An important part of character-building is putting off what
we want—delayed gratification. That's not a popular concept
for us addicts! We have trained ourselves to live for the quick
fix. There always has to be something in it for us. The payoff
for this recovery work is not immediate. Nor will it always
mean you'll get what you want or what you *think* you want.
You may be so stuck in trying to feed your happiness—*now!*—
that the work you say you are committed to in meetings, with
your sponsor, and to your loved ones does indeed often get
lost in your immaturity and self-centeredness.

We eventually must put our spiritual values first and material pleasures second if we're to find our real purpose. But
our society does not work this way. No commercial or marketing strategy tells people to put community and taking care
of self above material comfort. In fact, society's message is
the opposite: we're told that we can buy happiness, though it
never seems to happen. Over and over the ads show and tell
us that the most successful man has the coolest car, is the
sexiest, and has the most money. Whatever we have is never

enough, and that's a recipe for a sad and frustrating life. Most of all, though, Step Seven tells us the biggest reason true happiness has been elusive is because we've been far too self-reliant; we lacked humility and connection with others.

Becoming the man we would like to be, however, is easier said than done. "What kind of man *do* I want to be?" we ask ourselves. We don't really know because many of us had no good model. And this is another way the recovery community helps us. We can see, meet, and get to know men who have what we want. Other men show us through their behavior the man we can become. The vision of who we are can only be achieved through hard work, but choosing to "take our comfort" is an easy temptation. Many of us spend much of our adult lives, including many years in recovery, looking for the easier, softer way. We run from our pain and try to avoid facing our problems. We hide because we are afraid. Afraid of failing. Afraid of hard work. Even afraid of succeeding. We are afraid that our life will not turn out the way we want it to. We may even be given various opportunities simply because we are men, but until we come to believe in ourselves, in our abilities, and in our accomplishments, we will never feel good about ourselves. We will never be able to look at "the guy in the glass."

And so we seek comfort wherever and however we can find it. And sadly, that's often in the arms of our character defects because that's what we know—and sometimes all we know. These habits have built up over many years. Inevitably they fail us because no human power or material object can provide the comfort we crave. But we will indulge in character-building if we believe we will get something. *Twelve Steps and Twelve Traditions* states:

> With a proper display of honesty and morality, we'd stand a better chance of getting what we really wanted. But whenever we had to choose between character and comfort, the character-building was lost in the dust of our chase after what we thought was happiness. Seldom did we look at character-building as something desirable in itself, something we would like to strive for whether our instinctual needs were met or not. We never thought of making honesty, tolerance, and true love of man and God the daily basis of living.[1]

What an order! You may think you can't go through with it! But you can, and you'll have more help than you realize.

Bludgeoned into Humility

Step Seven is a partnership between you and your Higher Power. Your only part, after getting ready in Step Six, is humbly asking for your Higher Power's help. Yes, it's that "asking for help" idea again. As a man, you constantly have to challenge any "go it alone" attitude you may have throughout the Steps. Rob said:

> This Step is anti-machismo. The Steps, especially this one, snuff out machismo.

You do not do the heavy lifting in Step Seven—your Higher Power does—and that will probably be a difficult concept for you to accept. Rob continued, "I have to fully concede to myself that my Higher Power is the way to better myself as a man." As we discussed in Step Six, men are supposed to be the ones who fix everything—on our own. We are men for God's sake! You've probably told yourself, "If I can figure out what is wrong, then I can fix it and move on." You did this almost instinctually.

The practice of humility is not something that most of us identified with in men whom we saw as successful. Before you got into recovery, you probably never spent much time thinking about humility. Without humility, few addicts and alcoholics stay clean and sober; they find it difficult to summon up the faith to get through the really hard times. In humility, you are one among many—no better and no less than another. In humility, you do not have all of the answers, and you ought not feel that you should. You recognize that you do not always have to know how life is supposed to be. When Brian was talking about humility he said, "One of the best skills I acquired in recovery is the ability to say 'I don't know' when the answer eludes me."

In humility, you surrender to the fact that you are not the one in control. You recognize and accept exactly how powerless you are in so many areas of your life. Whenever you can let go of being in charge of fixing or removing a defect of character, then you are working Step Seven. Without humility, you'll continue to experience pain despite your constant attempts to avoid it.

Little by little we become wiser as we grow in our recovery. We begin to value and strive for humility without having to be beaten down by life. At last, we begin to see the pattern and that our attempts to live by self-sufficiency are keeping us miserable. Our ill-fated attempts to live using our old strategies have us constantly crashing into other people and ourselves. We want to use a hammer when we need a screwdriver; a drill when we need a saw. After living with incredible amounts of pain, our sobriety will reinforce the realization that drugs were only a symptom of an underlying cause, and that we—with our "self-will run riot"—were often the real cause.

Even though help is readily available to us, it's astonishing how easily we can repeatedly be brought to our knees by our pride, arrogance, and ignorance. What are you afraid of? Perhaps you're afraid of taking the risk of being yourself in a world that you view as hostile, or at least as having rejected you. Perhaps you fear letting go of your life so it can go where it naturally seems to be going rather than where you keep trying to force it to go. Perhaps you fear having to accept that you truly don't always have to be in control. This fear of yours is one of the greatest barriers to your growth and progress in recovery. When hiding behind pride, arrogance, and ignorance, your fear causes others much pain. Only humility can free you from the pain of living in this fear. Most of us do not embrace humility because we believe it's the pathway to peace and happiness; no, we embrace humility because we finally realize that we're all out of options. Paul said:

> *I did not join AA because it was a club I wanted to belong to. I joined because I had no other choice. You can go to treatment, a halfway house, and AA meetings but until you ask for help you will not begin your recovery. Admitting you don't know how to recover from alcoholism is true humility.*

The more we embrace humility in our lives the more we lose the worst parts of the masculine script. Juan talked about this:

> Some of the nurturing elements of being a human being are not put out as being a valued part of a masculine package by our popular culture. Stoic, hard, physical, dishonest . . . The lying, cheating, and dishonest male is put on a pedestal and put out there as a role model, which is troubling and disappointing.

Juan went on to say that AA has given him the ability to become accepting of his own masculinity and be "comfortable not adhering to societal norms." Juan is not the only man who sees this now. This transformation is exactly what Andy was talking about in Step Six when he spoke of the conflict between who he was as a person and how we was supposed to be and live as a man. Whether it is entitlement, pride, arrogance, stoicism, dishonesty, or any other defect of character, the humility we cultivate in Steps Six and Seven will allow our Higher Power to overcome them. They simply cannot exist in the same space as humility. In talking about humility, Kit said this:

> I didn't identify humility for what it was, rather [I saw it as] weakness, doubt, or indecision. Having practiced Step Seven, I now recognize how I can practice humility, that is, humanness, without self-recrimination or self-chastisement.

Sober Horse Thieves

Here's an old joke you'll hear in Twelve Step meetings: "What happens when you sober up a horse thief? You get a sober horse thief!"

A coworker once came to me to talk about her sister who was newly sober and struggling to feel comfortable attending and talking in Twelve Step meetings. She asked me about recovery and for ways that she might support her sister. About a month later, I asked her how her sister was doing, and she said she was okay. Yes, she had found a meeting. She had also apparently fallen in love. My coworker proceeded to tell me that her sister's new boyfriend, who was a "leader" of the meeting with twenty-five years of sobriety, was having sex with her sister (about twenty years his junior) at his other girlfriend's house while the girlfriend was working to pay for the rent and food. This same man talked about the virtues of the program in meetings and even instructed others how to work the Steps. This, to me, is a perfect description of a person *stuck* in recovery. Somehow, by the grace of God, he stays sober; yet, emotional maturity, the result of repeatedly working Steps Six and Seven, continues to elude him as he preaches the virtues and truths of the recovery program. He is a fifty-year-old boy. I explained to my coworker that this man neither represented mature recovery nor did he respect himself, women in recovery, or women in general. His behavior did not reflect the principles of recovery. We have an obligation to each other to not accept that kind of behavior, but it happens far too often without comment, let alone intervention.

We men in recovery suffer from unaddressed mental health issues, unresolved trauma, rage, gambling addiction, sex addiction, workaholism, and any number of spiritual maladies that eat at our souls—*in our sobriety.* When Steps Six and Seven introduce us to our pride, entitlement, arrogance, and so on, they also expose the other addictions and spiritual maladies that plague our recovery and that have been hiding deeper than we ever imagined.

I did not get on medication until I was eight years sober. I was not diagnosed with post-traumatic stress disorder until I was ten years sober. I did not begin to understand meditation until I was ten years sober. I had no idea how harmful my anger, rage, and abusiveness were to the lives of those I loved the most until I was eleven years sober. Looking back, I can see how often my Higher Power carried me through those difficult times. You must trust that you can live through this process, that you deserve to have a better life, and that you will be okay. If you are feeling stuck—when you are feeling stuck—don't try to go it alone. Ask for help and work the Steps. The same wisdom and simple daily actions that got you sober will continue to transform your life. On the other end of the pain you can find peace and hope, but it doesn't come free. You must do the work.

Happy, Joyous, and Free

Without question, recovery is an issue of life and death. Once you have been sober and attending meetings for a while, you'll realize one day the reality of the life-and-death struggle you are in because you will see some fine people who don't make it and some who will die. You'll be reminded that you have a disease and that taking good care of yourself offers you a chance to live a worthwhile life. But can you be "happy, joyous, and free" in sobriety when you're still driven by the fear and anxiety fed by your defects of character? You can't be. You won't be.

When you get tired of your suffering and turn your defects over to your Higher Power, your sobriety will open you to a whole new dimension. You will discover that the house you have lived in for the past five years has a second floor and a basement that you never knew existed. Then a third floor. Then more rooms on each floor, and even more floors! There is always room for more growth and more self-discovery, not to mention more joy and happiness, too!

Humbly Asking

Reggie's words reflect the essence of Step Seven:

Asking for help had previously been a sign of weakness for me . . . I finally accepted and recognized that I was not able to remove my defects of character myself . . . and that was a sign of strength illustrated by my growing relationship with my Higher Power.

When I imagine myself humbly asking God to remove my shortcomings, I am on bended knee, with my head down, in a very calm and soft voice, with no expectation of my wish being granted. I beseech my Higher Power to help me, like a servant asking his king for an incredible favor. Being a humble servant is the essence of recovery in the Twelve Steps. When you ask, you shall receive. Step Seven's promise of humility says that no unhappiness is too great to be lessened and no defect of character is more powerful than the spiritual solution of the Twelve Steps. You may feel overwhelmed. You may find yourself feeling as though the task before you is too great . . . and it will be so long as you persist in doing everything yourself. Humility for Andy means recognizing, once and for all, that "I do not have the power as a man to completely heal myself by myself; there has to be constant reliance on a power greater than me." When you enlist the help of your Higher Power and the Twelve Step community, you can move mountains—and you will!

STEP EIGHT

Made a list of all persons we had harmed,
and became willing to make amends to them all.

Step Eight was really powerful in that
it helped me realize that the shame
I had from how I had treated other
people was actually keeping me
tethered to my disease.

– JUAN –

When you put down the drugs or whatever addictive substance or process is destroying your life, you are left only with relationships. Steps Four and Five helped you begin to understand the role you played in creating the pain in your life and to share that realization with another human being. This was the beginning of the end of secrets and isolation. If you are to live free in this world, to make positive contributions to it, and to fully enjoy the fruits of recovery, you have to take your recovery beyond the narrow boundaries of your "property line." You need to step out into the community.

While it's true that many of us men find it difficult to show that we care about our relationships, every man I interviewed talked about how valuable relationships were to him. At the heart of Steps Eight and Nine lies a process that can help restore your belief that you deserve to rejoin the human community. Once you become more honest with yourself, you may discover that it's not that you don't want to be a part of the community again, but rather that you may not be sure you know how to do so, or if you even deserve this.

As you begin to work Step Eight and make your list, you'll quickly realize how many lives you've affected. You are not an island and never have been. In your addiction, you hurt many people, and that's a reality you cannot change. But being a man, as every single man I interviewed stated, is about taking responsibility. In Step Eight you take responsibility for your actions, past and present. The hope Step Eight promises is this: by being willing to face the people you've harmed, you gain the power to end the destructive cycle that has been eating away at all of your relationships.

Many men talked about the shame they felt for the wrongs they had committed because of their addictions, and about the damage they had caused to their relationships as a result. Juan mentioned several harms that haunted him until he'd completed these Steps. One episode was particularly moving, mostly because of the emotion he expressed as he recounted it so many years later:

Here's one incident that haunted me and that I've finally been able to forgive myself for. I was with a group of guys who would go hunting to pick fights. I remember breaking out a young man's teeth—literally smashing him in the face—and I turned and looked at my friend and said, "God, I think I broke my hand." He [the young man] looked up at me and said, "I think you broke my face." I think about that and the remorse . . .

Juan, like many men, talked about his "strong moral compass" that made his shame worse because he engaged in behavior he knew was wrong. Through Steps Eight and Nine, Reggie faced avoided DWIs and taxes. Charlie faced crimes he'd committed as a juvenile that had caused great destruction and bodily harm to others, such as burning down houses and blinding a man. Brandon had to face people from numerous businesses from which he had stolen. The list goes on. Yet, all of these men today both live in the community and are active contributors to it. No matter the wrongs you've committed, you, too, can rejoin the community. Step Eight will show you the way.

Tortured by Loneliness

Regardless of how we act on the outside, most of us are plagued by feelings of isolation and loneliness. And let's face it—many men do not talk about or admit to being lonely. Bill Wilson talked about the pain of the addict's loneliness in *Twelve Steps and Twelve Traditions:*

Almost without exception, alcoholics are tortured by loneliness. Even before our drinking got bad and people began to cut us off, nearly all of us suffered the feeling that we didn't quite belong. Either we were shy, and dared not draw near others, or we were noisy good fellows constantly craving attention and companionship, but never getting it—at least to our way of thinking.[1]

This quote resonated deeply with me the first time I read it early in my first year of sobriety. The men and women going to your meetings know this same loneliness. You truly are not alone.

At the root of our loneliness is that lie about ourselves we have discussed throughout this book telling us that we are fundamentally unlovable. By trying to hide the lie with the trappings of ego—money, success, arrogance, and so on—we constantly delude ourselves by thinking that if we build up the outside, it will fix the inside. It won't, and it never will. Peter talked about how his idea of what it means to be a real man had changed:

> Before recovery, a "real" man was the guy with the fancy sports car who had the corner office and the trophy wife . . . all the outside stuff . . . the material stuff. He was probably fairly detached, aloof, and smug. Women flocked to him. He never exposed his feelings. Now, after eight years of recovery, I realize that he's me! I spent a lifetime hating looking in the mirror. Today, the guy who looks back at me in that mirror is a member of the community. He's kind, he's considerate of others, he's tolerant, and he's loving. The corner office is irrelevant today.

Step Eight is men saying, "I don't want to be lonely. I don't want to live with this lie anymore. I need you and I need your love."

Here are what might be some very scary questions: What if every negative judgment you put on yourself might actually be false? What if you really were a good person, capable of loving and being loved? What if you do deserve to be a part of the human community as much as anyone else? Well, you are . . . and you do! Everyone faces feelings of self-doubt, and Step Eight can help you find courage to face and share your doubts about yourself with others.

It's Just a List

Bill W. and the other first members of Alcoholics Anonymous were very smart when they created Steps Eight and Nine. Step Eight asks you to be very thoughtful as you move ahead. Be patient and don't rush. Make the list. Discuss the list with your sponsor. Look at each name on the list and talk about that person with your sponsor to understand as well as you can exactly what is your best course of action. Know your motives. Find the willingness to make amends and figure out the best order in which to do them. Pray for guidance and humility. Recovery is not a race. You do not get a prize for finishing first!

You may also hesitate to make this list, or think you don't really need one. You may resist putting a certain person on your list. You may want these relationships to heal but let your fear of facing them delay or stop you. Fear of conflicts that could arise. Fear that they may actually want to have you back in their lives, or that they might not want you back! Fear that they might not forgive or love you, or fear that they will.

While fear often accompanies our efforts to make amends, you will find strength when you turn to your recovery group and your Higher Power. The faith you gain throughout this process is essential as you bring your recovery out into the world. Yes, you'll feel vulnerable and afraid, so you have to trust that your Higher Power is going to take care of you each and every step of the way. You are finally learning how to be in relationships.

It's also helpful to remember that at this point, you're only creating a list.

Know Your Motives

My sponsor, Eric, helped me understand that one of the most important and useful aspects of Step Eight—to understand your motives for wanting to make amends to someone—will ensure that Step Nine is done with integrity. Why do you think you have harmed this person? In what way? What are your motivations? In other words, what do you hope to get out of this process? Why make this amend now? Are you approaching making amends from a spirit of service? Is making the amend about you, or about them? *The fact is, it is not about you!* You will hear this caution over and over again throughout your recovery, but it's never more important than when you are working Steps Eight and Nine. It's been all about you for far too long!

Understanding your motives is important for many reasons. Perhaps the most important is that it will help you avoid causing further harm to an individual or a relationship. We tend to put people on our amends list for a number of reasons—some good, some not. Sometimes we pretend to have one motive for making an amend while still hiding the true one—to get back together with an ex, to punish someone, to get an apology, and so on. If you are not honest with yourself about your motives, you will most certainly compromise the integrity of the amend. The point of reentering the world is to be able to clean up your messes, not make more. Work with your sponsor as you ask yourself these questions, and be clear about why you owe each person an amend. Nothing is more important than clarity in your actions if you want the community to invite you back.

What about Me?

Yes, and what about you? Should *you* be on your Step Eight list? Perhaps. Have you hurt yourself? Absolutely. You have abandoned yourself and your values in your addictions. You have been perhaps the biggest source of punishment and ridicule in your life. You have put yourself in situations and relationships you would have never allowed a friend to experience. Yes, clearly you have harmed yourself, and you need to understand and admit that many of the mistakes you made wouldn't have happened had you not been active in your addiction. Your recovery and your commitment to it are two of the greatest amends you can make to yourself. Once you've done so, you'll come to believe that you can face anything. You can do anything. You'll be able to take your recovery to the next level, where you can truly be "happy, joyous, and free"!

The longer you stay sober, the more you will hear other men talk about putting yourself on the list. Often, these are men with years of recovery who have attempted to live in their own skin while still hating themselves. Now is the time when you can—and must—pay attention to the ways you harm yourself on a daily basis. How do you treat yourself? How do you talk to yourself, and how do you take care of yourself?

At this point in your recovery, there's no reason you should still be walking through the world oblivious to the effect you have had on others and on yourself. You should be able to see the impact of your behavior on others—and accept that you are responsible for how you deal with your feelings and how you act on a daily basis.

Though many of your relationships will likely now be restored and solid, you may still find yourself wondering if people really do like or care about you. You may still criticize and insult yourself when you make mistakes. You may still struggle to be in your own skin. You feel that you're "fakin' it to make it" a little too much. That's when *you* go on the list. Peter talked about his experience when he was five years sober:

> Some of those tapes were still running, and I couldn't accept that I really was doing the right things and putting the effort in. That tape was still saying, "You are still a phony." It doesn't matter if I was or not.

Once you begin to see how you harm yourself, you will begin to have compassion for yourself. You will begin to see how that self-abuse has been at the root of how you treat others. The next level of healing work to be done then becomes clearer. This is when you get to fall in love with yourself. Yes,

I did use the words *fall in love with yourself.* It may sound stupid or crazy but how can you ever truly love another if you are constantly struggling against yourself? You can't. When you have known the depth of self-loathing experienced by so many of us, you need to fall in love with yourself—or at the very least learn to like yourself. It's unlikely that you'll ever be happy if you don't.

The Beginning of the End of Isolation

Most of us have struggled with relationships because we were not taught how to have relationships, and our addiction didn't help! Step Eight challenges you not only to heal your current relationships, but to face your past and heal the relationships that have already been scarred by your addiction. Step Eight reinforces the importance of forming and keeping solid, healthy relationships. It introduces the very real possibility of forgiveness—from others as well as self-forgiveness. Juan was convinced that recovery couldn't last without self-forgiveness:

It starts with that unification of self, and that's huge. In time, I found that I really was taking responsibility for my behavior. For me now, the forgiveness of self is very closely linked to the forgiveness and acceptance of others around me.

If we are entitled to anything, it would be the gift of forgiveness. Steps Nine and Ten will offer you the freedom and opportunity to repair those relationships and to experience the reality of forgiveness in a most profound way.

All human beings are social creatures. We value and need

relationships. That desire to connect is everywhere, even in the darkest bar or the grittiest part of town. That desire to connect is still alive even on the bleakest days of your addiction or on the darkest day of your sobriety. Men want to be with others. We may not have learned how to be in relationships in the healthiest way, but we still want them. We may not be the best at asking for what we need, but we still have needs.

We regain our confidence in our ability to connect when we interact with one another before, during, and after meetings. We express ourselves and our affection for one another in a way that we may not have thought possible. We are reminded that, without meaningful relationships, life is miserable. With our recovery community, we can be "a part of" again. We can give ourselves the chance to feel, perhaps for the first time in our lives, that we're part of a strong link in the human chain of connection. When you commit yourself to thoroughly and honestly working Step Eight, you move further down the path away from isolation and shame toward the healing power of loving relationships with other people and your Higher Power.

STEP NINE

*Made direct amends to such people wherever possible,
except when to do so would injure them or others.*

**Step Nine—the toughest one for me—
showed me that to clean up my side
of the street was the single most
freeing action I have ever taken.**

– KIT –

Step Nine gives men in the Twelve Step community something that men outside of that community too often do not
get: the opportunity to take responsibility for the harms we
have caused others. In recovery, we have begun to value
our relationships again. But making amends is not about re-
building relationships. We're not doing this Step to force our
way back into other people's lives. We can't expect anything
from the people we have harmed just because we're making amends. As Peter said, "Sometimes the most important
thing I can do in making amends is to carry out the process
and then leave that person alone." You have no control over
the outcome of any amend. Some people may not forgive

you, and you'll just have to accept that. It's a choice they get to make, not you. Given that, you should always be willing to go to any length to restore love to broken relationships, regardless of the outcome. Step Nine offers you the opportunity to take responsibility, clean up the messes you have made as best you can, and then let go.

In making amends you will experience forgiveness, and part of that is accepting that you cannot change the past. We seldom see the impact our harmful actions have on ourselves. Many men are haunted for years by violent acts they committed when they were young and trying to prove that they were men. Because those actions violated their core values, they used the pain of those actions (often unknowingly) to punish themselves. Brandon addressed this when he said, "Making amends is realizing that the harms you have caused are forgivable, and you are not doomed to being 'less than' because of them."

No matter what you have done, you deserve forgiveness whether or not you think you do. If I had waited to make amends until I felt deserving of forgiveness, I would never have done them. I knew I wanted to be a better man and to have better relationships, even though I didn't know how to make that happen. The answer was in simply taking the action. Forgiveness comes as a result of taking the action.

For many men, forgiveness of self comes as an unexpected gift when doing Step Nine. Juan said:

> *To me, forgiveness in the Eighth and Ninth Steps was about forgiveness of self. I was vicious and brutal to myself, but at the*

end of it, I had come to accept my own past behavior . . . and with that, I began to feel whole again. Really understanding and owning something I did, processing it as a whole, and taking a specific action to make that behavior right.

When you finally face the experiences from the past that you're so ashamed of and then truly accept responsibility for your behavior, you experience freedom. Juan went on to say that while forgiveness of others is valuable, forgiveness of self is essential to recovery. Charlie realized that after making some of his most difficult amends, his past was not who he was anymore.

Facing Conflict

Making amends may also involve conflict—real or imagined. While this may frighten you, be assured that you're not the only man who's felt this way. As with any of your problems, the best action you can take is talking with your sponsor or other men in the program about your fears. Be as honest as you can, and remember that your fear is not unmanly. Your fear means you care—about yourself, about others, and about your relationships. And it's a sign of your healing.

Many of us were never taught healthy ways to address conflict. Chances are you go to "fight or flight" mode far too quickly, and that has caused much of the strain you now seek to address in your relationships. As a result, many of us concluded that simply avoiding problems might be the best way to deal with them. We are afraid that if we face our problems, we will end up in a confrontation—possibly even a physical one. As you make amends, you'll begin to realize that they're teaching you how to heal from conflict. If you are fortunate, those you've harmed will tell you about the effect your past behaviors had on them. You will learn how to sit and hear someone's anger and hurt without getting defensive and reacting. You will begin to realize that the fight or flight reaction that's been controlling your relationships no longer controls you. You'll begin to see that many of your fears were unwarranted. Your confidence will grow as you begin to stand firm in the face of the discomfort that is a part of all relationships. You can get through any amend that you and your sponsor determine is appropriate.

Mature Amends: The Spiritual Life Is Not a Theory

In your excitement about your recovery, you may go into this Step with your eyes closed—or rather with your eyes focused on yourself. Once again, remember you are not the focus. Since you've probably spent much of your life thinking mostly of yourself, you will need some time and practice before you can put yourself in the place of another person and have his or her best interests at heart when making an amend. Dave said:

> I want to think I operate in a vacuum, and any pain caused by my behavior is mine alone. I now realize that I live among other people who care about me—and who have made themselves vulnerable to me.

Talking with someone to whom you're making an amend is far different than talking in meetings or to your sponsor. You will be facing people you've harmed, and in doing so you'll bring up painful memories—not just for you, but for them, too. This Step says that you make amends "except when to do so would injure them or others." That part of the Step is *very* important. Again, making an amend is not just about you. If you have any doubts that an amend might affect someone, talk with your sponsor before moving ahead.

For many of us, saying "I am sorry" is easy; changing our behavior is much more difficult! Many men, and perhaps you, too, have learned that saying "I am sorry" is just part of the act: you act out, you are caught or feel guilty, and then you give an insincere apology with no awareness of how your behavior affected that person. As a child, you might have been told to apologize to a sibling you fought with or to a fellow student whom you had hurt. The adults in your life were trying to teach you a valuable lesson about conflict resolution and the importance of facing up to the harm you caused other people. You were to say "I'm sorry" not because you had been caught, but because you had done something that had hurt someone else. What you weren't taught, or what you refused to accept, is that you were also supposed to change your behavior!

Telling someone you're sorry is meaningless if not coupled with a change in how you interact with that person. You have no business making amends if you are still doing the same behavior that caused the harm.

Think about the relationships you have. What negative behaviors continue? Are you using "I'm sorry" to fool yourself into thinking that you have genuine remorse for your behavior? Are your apologies just an attempt to avoid trouble? Are they just another attempt to manipulate others to feel sorry for you and let you off the hook?

Many of the people on the other end of your immature and self-centered behavior may be enabling you—intentionally or unintentionally. They might fall for your charm and say that your apology is enough. They may just want to see the best in you. After a while, though, no one is doing you any favor by not confronting you and saying, for example, "That 'I'm sorry' isn't good enough anymore. I don't believe you are really sorry. Stop treating me that way, and then I will know that you are sincere."

Whether or not someone confronts you, you are ultimately responsible for your behavior. Your task now is to pay close attention to how you affect others, particularly when you are feeling emotional. The problem lies with you, not them.

Your Real Purpose

Making amends is also one of the first opportunities for you to be of service in the program. For years, you served only your addiction and yourself. The Big Book is very clear that our "real purpose is to fit ourselves to be of maximum service to God and the people about us."[1] The Big Book does not really talk about your needs or what you should expect from life. You probably spent a lot of your life wondering how other people were going to make your life better. You may have even spent much time in recovery focused on you, your feelings, and how the world affects you. Constantly wondering if you will have enough of this, that, or the other thing. And you still felt miserable.

Waiting for something or someone to make you whole is an exhausting way to live. Learning to be of service to another human being is the great lesson of recovery. When you go out of your way to be of service to another human being, you feel better. Only you can make you whole.

Step Nine will also show you that broken relationships can be repaired, that people love you and see the best in you, even in your worst times, and that forgiveness depends more on you than others. Even if some relationships are not reclaimed as a result of your work in Step Nine, you can still live with the knowledge that you have faced your fears and taken ownership for the harms you have caused others. You will understand that you are not unique. You do not have to live alone or filled with a quiet desperation. The world, despite its problems and challenges, really is a wonderful place, and the promises of recovery really can come true for you! Kit said it very well:

Emotional and spiritual freedoms involve giving up that which is beyond me, owning up to who and what I am, making up with those I have harmed, and keeping up with my personal growth.

STEP TEN

Continued to take personal inventory
and when we were wrong promptly admitted it.

I can face each day with the understanding
that my manhood and strength are tied to
my ability to admit my shortcomings and
grow through that process.

- REGGIE -

The unexamined life is not worth living.

-SOCRATES -

Charlie called Step Ten "the most male Step" because it stays focused and grounded "through daily spiritual inventory and discipline." Step Ten lays the foundation for a life worth living by showing us how to create a consistent pattern of self-examination—ideally on a daily basis. The life of an addict is the classic unexamined life. You live from day to day, a slave to your addiction. Your life is, at best, secondary to getting your fix. You do not examine your life while active in your addiction except for two reasons: to continue (or increase) your addiction or, due to the consequences of your addiction, you need to figure out how to get out of whatever problem you are in. So, you get sober. You go to meetings, work with your sponsor, and study and practice the Steps. You begin to feel comfortable in your recovery.

What do you do, however, with all the feelings you keep having? How do you act outside of your meetings? How do you feel when you are alone or when the spotlight is not on you? These questions should and can serve as guideposts on your path to sobriety and wisdom. You have proven that you can get sober and that's wonderful. Now, at last, you can build on that foundation to create the life you want. Are you willing to do the daily work necessary to stay sober?

When you lose touch with your feelings, old thought patterns can again begin to drive your actions and push you toward unhealthy anger or inappropriate emotional responses, such as rage, abusiveness, or harming others. It can lead you closer to isolation, depression, or acting out in any number of ways.

The purpose of Step Ten is to help you learn to look at your own behavior as a detached, nonjudgmental observer. With constant practice and compassionate discipline we learn to accept what we see—everything. This practice is not only daily but is meant to become a part of the rest of our lives. As *Alcoholics Anonymous* says:

> . . . *We continue to take personal inventory to set right any new mistakes as we go along . . . Our next function is to grow in under-*

standing and effectiveness. This is not an overnight matter. It should continue for our lifetime.[1]

The practice of self-searching—taking a personal inventory—is an essential tool for your recovery that can and should challenge you on a moment-to-moment basis to pay attention to what you're doing. Step Ten introduces you to practicing the spiritual discipline of awareness of what's happening both inside of you and around you. It asks you to take responsibility for whatever you are experiencing in a given moment. It's asking you to be aware of yourself. As Reggie said, "Step Ten is a wonderful daily reminder that I am fallible and must face the world through constant and fearless self-examination."

Taking a personal inventory on a regular basis will help you recognize how you are responding to life and to others at any given moment. Kit talked about this:

Step Ten grants me permission to try and succeed or try and fail, regardless of the outcome. Each day becomes another day to practice my life. With each success, my responsibility to share with others increases, while with each failure my responsibility increases to own my part in the situation and to share that with others, too.

Whatever we feed grows. When you feed the part of you that is petty, immature, reactive, hypersensitive, and self-centered, then you strengthen that part of you. On the other hand, you can also choose to feed the part of you that is loving, mature, generous, calm, tolerant, and other-centered. In reality, we all feed different parts of ourselves at different times in different situations with different people. Which one are you more likely to want to feed? Which one have you been feeding for years, if not decades? Which one are men more likely to feed? Of course, habits like these simply won't change overnight. This is why we call these daily efforts "practice." That malnourished and weak best self within you will not gain strength right away, but it will eventually so long as you continue to feed it.

Focus on Yourself

The rigorous self-study of Step Ten is easier said than done for most of us because we have become masters of observing others but rarely ourselves. If you pause and pay attention to your inner dialogue, you will notice how often throughout the day you judge and blame others for whatever current problem or upset you are experiencing. Focusing on others' behavior is not only ill-advised, it's simply not useful. You are wasting your energy having conversations with others in your head. You assume you know their motives, and you judge them based on certain situations and behaviors. Do you think you have any ability to control their behavior? Despite the uselessness of this, you will still most likely find yourself focusing on others far more often than you would like.

Practice distancing yourself from others' behaviors. As you do this, you'll begin to realize that your responses have to do with your perception and how you interpret their behavior. You will come to see that their behavior need not bother you. Letting it upset you only ruins your day, not theirs! *Alcoholics Anonymous* says it well:

We realized that the people who wronged us were perhaps spiri-
tually sick. Though we did not like their symptoms and the way
these disturbed us, they, like ourselves, were sick too . . . We can-
not be helpful to all people, but at least God will show us how to
take a kindly and tolerant view of each and every one.[2]

You could describe these efforts, which stretch us emotionally in ways that may seem unbearable and unreasonable,
as the pains of growing up. Yes, recovery is our chance to
grow up and, as West said, "put our big-boy pants on." We become the best men we can be, regardless of our age. Step Ten
gives us the tools to move closer to this goal on a daily basis.

A Spiritual Axiom

When I first became sober, I had no idea that my reactions were not completely out of my control. I had become
so separated from my feelings that all anyone had to do was
push the right button and I would react. I might as well have
been a robot because I was certainly acting like one! Push a
button, get a response. My first sponsor, Bill, suggested that
I read Step Ten in *Twelve Steps and Twelve Traditions* and
pay particular attention to the following saying: "It is a spiritual axiom that every time we [you] are disturbed, no matter
what the cause, there is something wrong *with us* [you]."[3]

As a man, I suffered through pretending that I was okay
because I could never let on to how confused I was. I was
just one more pretender in a sea of pretenders, all pretending that we were not pretending. I was the funny guy. The
happy-go-lucky guy. The smart guy. I needed to be okay. And

so I had convinced myself that if I was disturbed, it was because there was something wrong with the other person.

Finally, however, the message of the Twelve Steps began to seep into my brain. Maybe it was possible that whenever I was disturbed, it was because there was something wrong with me. I finally began to think that understanding this concept could actually help me!

The beauty of this concept can elude us for many years. But pay attention, and it will be a reminder that any time you are focused on someone else's behavior, you have an opportunity to look at yourself. The statement says *every time* (not just occasionally) you are disturbed, something is wrong with you. That statement also applies when you have been harmed by another human being, too—past or present. It says *every time,* and that means in every instance.

The amount of freedom and power that can grow from applying this idea to every event in your life is immense. The wisdom you'll gain can help you cultivate a healthy sense of power in your life. You can finally move from just reacting to life to responding thoughtfully to life. You'll stop feeling like a puppet under the control of some hidden master as you begin consciously making choices and understanding your motivation and responsibility for them.

Accurate Self-Appraisal

As with Step Four, working Step Ten without being compassionate with yourself can lead to self-abuse. When you get to Step Ten, be aware that you will have difficulty being appropriately tough on yourself and appropriately loving toward yourself. We need to learn what it means to be able to *accurately* appraise ourselves, and that is not something many, if any, of us were taught. The key word here is *accurately,* which means that you see yourself fairly. You have taken notice of what you have done well as much as where you have been in error. You have been appropriately hard on yourself without falling into either of the extremes— self-abuse or irresponsibility. One of the hallmarks of recovery for men is learning how to be *appropriately* hard on ourselves—something that's eluded many of us, particularly while we were active in our addictions.

A lot of us focus on this particular part of Step Ten: admitting when you are wrong. While regularly taking your personal inventory, you will see times when you have been wrong. Contrary to what many men think, Step Ten's purpose is not to constantly catch yourself making mistakes. Doing Step Ten regularly will instead help you become more aware of your thinking and behavior on a moment-to-moment basis. You will begin to recognize when you are living well. Yes, you will see your progress. You will begin to focus on and see both what you're doing well and what you still need to work on. This process of taking our inventory will blossom into a way for us to see where we put forth our best motives, our best thoughts, and our best actions as much as any of the inevitable mistakes we make as we continue to grow. *Twelve Steps and Twelve Traditions* is quite clear about this and reflects Bill W.'s and AA's own development and growth in this area. This concept challenges any of us who think Twelve Step inventories are supposed to be negative. Not true at all. Always balance the ledger! For most of us, the challenge is seeing what we have done well and giving ourselves credit for the progress we are making.

Step Ten is constantly referred to as a *practice* because you are going to make mistakes, and you should be persistent nonetheless. You will beat yourself up. You will let yourself skate on certain offenses. You will blow off a significant accomplishment. As you learn how to practice Step Ten, ask a sponsor and your close friends in recovery to give you objective feedback about your self-assessment. A great gift for you on your new path: Progress not perfection. Look for it! Embrace it! Turn to it over and over! That little saying will help save your life!

Awareness

Here's the essence of Step Ten's unfolding process: you learn emotional awareness and how to take care of yourself. This is a wonderful gift but one that you'll need some time to fully appreciate. You may never find yourself sitting in a meeting and saying, "I am learning emotional awareness. Isn't that wonderful?" Chances are you won't say to your sponsor, "Thank you for helping me to grow in my emotional awareness." Instead, one day you will, for example, find yourself talking about how angry you were in some situation only to catch yourself and say, "I wasn't really feeling angry anyway. I was feeling hurt and afraid, and I took it out on her." That is emotional growth. That is powerful.

The greater your awareness, the more prompt you can be in admitting when you are wrong. Brian said, "It is incredibly freeing to admit a mistake, to grow from it, and to move on." You realize that admitting you are wrong is only you acknowledging your humanness. It means nothing about your competency, maturity, or worth as a man.

You will also realize that the concept of harm is broad. You'll see that much of the harm you have caused others began with the harm you did to yourself. You don't ignore the harm you caused others. Instead you look at the negativity in your daily conversations with yourself. You step outside of yourself and notice how well you are practicing the principles of recovery during each day. Every time you sacrifice your values just to fit in with others, you harm yourself. Every time you violate any of your values, you harm yourself. From these harms, you will begin to feel a general dissatisfaction with the world that will affect all of your interactions with others. Resolve this dissatisfaction by practicing positive self-talk. Peace and happiness come from within, and they cannot exist when your inner world is filled with chaos. As time passes and you continue to work at your recovery, you may eventually be able to interrupt a certain habit or thought pattern while it is still in your head. That is emotional awareness: the powerful and freeing benefit of Step Ten. You learn to take your own inventory and to be entirely responsible for your life. You can do this. As you walk this path, you'll grow and be transformed. Many men before you have succeeded, and they will help you.

Ϋ

STEP ELEVEN

Sought through prayer and meditation to improve
our conscious contact with God as we understood Him,
praying only for knowledge of His will for us
and the power to carry that out.

Learning and practicing both prayer
and meditation is my most important gift
in keeping my authentic male self.

– CHARLIE –

Step Eleven tells us that the way we grow in our relationship with our Higher Power is through the use of prayer
and meditation. Many of the men I interviewed for this book
spoke about some familiarity with prayer before recovery
that has developed into a genuine connection. Dan J. talked
about how his communication with his Higher Power has
matured:

Prayer has changed a lot for me over the years. I went from recit-
ing a lot of established prayers like the Third Step prayer to hav-
ing a more personal connection to my Higher Power. I still use
the prayers, but now I also talk to God. I ask for courage, strength,
and willingness. I express my gratitude for the things I have in my

life. I am no longer using the "Oh God, if you get me out of this one, I'll never do it again!" technique.

The wisdom of the program tells us that our growth in sobriety is built on the growth of our relationship with our Higher Power, whatever that may be. Reggie said, "My Higher Power has become a silent, powerful, and constant presence in my life."

By this point in your Twelve Step journey, you have most likely become comfortable with the idea of having a Higher Power in your life. In Step Eleven, you now begin to nurture your relationship with your Higher Power. If you have been paying close attention to the guidance in the literature and to your friends in the Twelve Step community, you have been working with your Higher Power throughout this process. You have likely come to see that this power greater than you is very real, and that positive and practical effects come from acknowledging its existence in your life. Step Eleven guides you in how you can use prayer and meditation to improve your conscious contact with your Higher Power, and in doing so your life will be further transformed.

Santa Claus

My sponsor Eric was fond of telling me that I often seemed to get my Higher Power and Santa Claus confused. He knew that I believed that if I was good, then life was supposed to be good, but if life was bad, I must have done something wrong. When I got sober I still carried a lot of the immature stories I had made up about God when I was a boy. Those stories were a big part of how I related to God, part of my conscious contact. Dan J. said:

> *I came into AA pissed off that God had made me an alcoholic. I swore I was agnostic and that God had abandoned me. I gave up on God and thought religion was a joke. The funny thing was that I never stopped believing in God; I just convinced myself that he did not love me.*

Like Dan J. and many of the other men I interviewed, I had confused my Higher Power with Santa Claus. Eric was right! Even worse, like Dan J., I saw myself in an abusive relationship with God! I had taken my experience growing up in a violent alcoholic home and turned it into the foundation for how I saw life.

Before going on, stop and take a few minutes to think about and answer the following questions:

- *What comes to mind when you think of your Higher Power? Of God?*
- *What stories about your Higher Power have you made up?*
- *What pain from your childhood or adult life have you turned over to your Higher Power? What was the result?*
- *What haven't you turned over yet?*

The previous questions will help you begin to better understand the concept you have of your Higher Power—not just the one you give lip-service to in meetings. When you begin to see your Higher Power as a loving and caring Higher Power you will be able to face even the most tragic circumstances of life in a new, positive, and constructive way.

Improving Your Conscious Contact

Your relationship with your Higher Power, like any other relationship, works to the degree that you devote your time and attention to it. If you go four months without talking to a friend, you won't be nearly as connected as you'd be if you spoke once a week. If you called that friend only when you wanted something, what would be the quality of that friendship? If you avoided dealing with any conflict in that relationship, how much trust would exist? If you are not honest in your relationships, no one will really know you, and that will only feed the deep sense of loneliness that you have probably fought all of your life. The same logic applies to your relationship with your Higher Power: as you improve your conscious contact with your Higher Power, you realize more and more that there is nothing that you cannot turn over to or share with your Higher Power. In fact, the openness and intimacy we create in our relationship with our Higher Power helps in all of our other relationships.

One day, while driving in my car, I was thinking about a relationship in which I was having a particularly difficult time. I had just discovered that the woman I was dating had a pretty serious addiction problem of her own. I was scared and had no idea what to do with my intense feelings of fear. I started talking to my Higher Power, whom I choose to call God. As I began speaking about my frustration, I felt anger welling up inside of me. Then, I began to yell and curse at God. Looking back now, I can see that moment marked a crucial turning point in my relationship with God. I realized that day that I could bring everything to God, no matter how messy, and give it to God to take care of. That was what "turning it over" really meant. On that day my relationship with God was transformed. I realized that my relationship with God was like any other relationship, and that I needed to be as honest in it as I could be.

When you share your whole self with your Higher Power, you strengthen your conscious contact with it. Keeping problems and concerns from your Higher Power inhibits your relationship. Equally important, you are keeping these things from yourself as well. When you hold yourself back, you'll feel more distant and disconnected. Even when you talk to your Higher Power about not feeling close to your Higher Power, you're still improving your conscious contact. When you talk to your Higher Power about your doubt that it exists or is even listening to you, you're improving your conscious contact. Every time you turn to your Higher Power—no matter how you are feeling and what you are saying—you are feeding the relationship.

If You Seek, You Shall Find

Addicts are often described as people using material means to find a spiritual solution. In the depths of our addiction, when life no longer seems tolerable, we turn to *something* for help. The noted psychiatrist, Carl Jung, pointed out in a letter to Bill Wilson that it was no coincidence that the Latin word for alcohol was *spiritus* ("you use the same word for the highest religious experience as well as for the most depraving poison") and that the addiction to alcohol "was the equivalent on a low level of the spiritual thirst of your being for wholeness . . . the union with God."[1]

As we saw in Step Two, the search for a Higher Power is a fundamental part of the human experience: your search for meaning, for something greater than you to guide you in this world. Whatever "it" is and however you describe it, this search has been an elemental part of the human journey as long as humans walked on this earth. Charlie said, "I was raised Catholic, lived as an atheist, and ultimately came to put my relationship with Love first." Step Eleven can help you reclaim and strengthen that relationship once and for all and to make it as personal as you want it to be.

Prayer

The first tool for improving conscious contact with the god of your understanding is prayer. Every man I interviewed spoke about how prayer has become a central practice in his daily life. Stop for a moment and think about what prayer means to you. Do you, or have you ever, prayed? Who taught you about prayer? What exactly is prayer? Does it bring up positive or negative feelings? Do you pray for specific outcomes? Why do you pray?

The creation of our prayer life in recovery often starts the same way: many of us pray because everyone we respect in the rooms of recovery talks about how important prayer is to their sobriety. While the traditional practice of prayer almost always includes an element of seeking guidance from a Higher Power, some men began their prayer life in a fairly immature way by trying to advance their own agenda. The Big Book and *Twelve Steps and Twelve Traditions* offer you several useful prayers. The prayer that is contained in Step Eleven itself is also very simple. Given our often immature orientation to prayer when we first get sober, the founders of AA made it easy: pray only for knowledge of God's will and the power to carry it out. *Alcoholics Anonymous* explains:

> *As we go through the day we pause, when agitated or doubtful, and ask for the right thought or action. We constantly remind ourselves we are no longer running the show, humbly saying to ourselves many times each day "Thy will be done." We are then in much less danger of excitement, fear, anger, worry, self-pity, or foolish decisions. We become much more efficient. We do not tire so easily, for we are not burning up energy foolishly as we did when we were trying to arrange life to suit ourselves.*[2]

When men first begin praying in sobriety, the best prayer is for God's will. Why? Because so many of our own words are wrapped up in "self," in what we think we need or deserve. Praying only for God's will to be done is always an effective prayer that you can turn to throughout your recovery. Reggie said, "My days are repeatedly punctuated by prayer and brief requests for God's will to be understood."

You may have been in a meeting or elsewhere, or found yourself saying, "God is telling me this" or "I know this is God's will for me." That may be, but these thoughts may also prove to be "well-intentioned unconscious rationalizations" as Bill Wilson calls them in *Twelve Steps and Twelve Traditions.*[3] Prayer is your thought, your agenda, and your words. As a result, a lot of prayer is talking *at* your Higher Power with little to no intention of listening.

Kit talked about what prayer used to be for him:

I prayed that people, situations, outcomes, conditions, and so on would be as I would have them. I was perpetually in a state of self-seeking and self-centered prayer.

We can pray simply to hear ourselves talk and convince ourselves that we are humbling ourselves to the mystery of life when in truth, we are just staying stuck in our heads, in our own reality.

As you grow in your recovery, your relationship with prayer will evolve.

What Dan J. described above happens to many men. But we go from using our Higher Power as a 9-1-1 operator to having a friend or companion to whom we can talk. We can learn intimacy in our conversations with our Higher Power. We can learn to trust in the unseen wisdom of the universe. And sometimes as our prayer life evolves it becomes even simpler, and we return to what we were shown early on. Quinn said it very succinctly:

I do not use prayers to petition for favors beyond acceptance. Thy will be done.

Prayer Is Constant

Here is another way to look at this: all thought is prayer. Does that seem oversimplified? Perhaps, but this perspective is helpful for several reasons. First, it brings prayer down to a very human and accessible level. For most of us, prayer has had an association with religion. But prayer can very simply be the way you turn your thoughts to that which is good; you do not have to pray to anything or anyone. Second, this idea allows us to see prayer as a constant part of our lives. At any moment you can turn your thoughts toward your Higher Power, Love, Gratitude, or whatever you want to call it. At any moment, you can think good thoughts about a person or a situation. What you focus on is completely under your control. Prayer by this definition can also be negative. For example, you might find yourself sitting in a meeting and judging what someone is saying. You then have an excellent opportunity to train your mind to hold a greater sense of gratitude, positivity, and peace. As Rob said:

Prayer has become the most important aspect of my daily life. It keeps me centered and focused on what is important to me. When I get away from daily prayer, I begin to take everything back to myself and become more selfish and ungrateful. Through my life experiences currently and in the past, the importance of prayer is continually confirmed. I truly receive guidance and inner clarity through this practice.

In the midst of pain and suffering, you are still free to focus on what you want: the positive or the negative. The more accustomed you are to having peace and happiness in your life, and to believing that you deserve to have them, the more quickly you will catch your negative thoughts. Once you're aware of them, of course, you can then turn your mind toward the positive. Brandon said, "I feel centered and reminded of the important things when I pray, and it is a helpful tool to feel grateful."

Prayer costs you nothing. No one can prevent you from praying, and nobody can take it away from you. Imagine that—you hold one of the most powerful tools for creating your happiness, and it's always available. Every thought you pray is one step closer or further from your very own happiness. Throughout the Steps you are told that the outside world is not what is making you miserable. It is your attitude, your perception, and how you are living your life. It is *you*. Both the happiness you have sought for so long and one of the greatest channels to get you there have been available to you all along.

Finally, Dave talked about approaching prayer from a different perspective. "The main idea is that you thank your Higher Power in the present moment for all of the support you are receiving for that which you are still hoping to achieve or accomplish." This is not a self-centered "Santa Claus" prayer, however, that requires a specific outcome. These are prayers of thanks that focus our attention. An example would be me saying, before having written this chapter, "Thank you God for giving me the words, ideas, and inspiration to write the chapter on Step Eleven."

Many of us don't question the negative thoughts we have about our life. We seldom question the fear-based outcomes we imagine. Yet, encourage us to be loving and hopeful toward ourselves and we are quickly tempted to laugh the idea off or think it silly or childish. Encourage us to pray as though that which we are working toward has already happened and we may feel as though we are being selfish or arrogant. Or we are afraid. What if what we pray for does not happen? What if our Higher Power isn't really helping? This is the very essence of faith: *what if?* Faith is a state of mind as much as anything; a tool that you can use. Sages from throughout history confirm that prayer is the bedrock of their awareness and the fullness in which they live. For me, this returns us to the simple truth I've found in working Step Two: "All is well."

Gratitude

The idea of gratitude could be included in a discussion of all the Steps. Every man in Twelve Step recovery who has been sober for an extended time knows that gratitude is an essential part of stable and long-term recovery. Brian spoke about gratitude this way:

I try to remember to thank God for the blessings I have been given. I once heard that one should not pray when it is raining if they are not willing to pray when the sun shines.

And a recovery saying states, "A truly grateful person does not relapse." I cannot overstate the importance of gratitude in cultivating happiness in your life. All the men I talked to said that learning the practice of gratitude has been essential to maintaining their sobriety. The fourteenth-century mystic, Meister Eckhart, wrote that if the only prayer you ever utter is "thank you," that is enough.

In early sobriety, gratitude is often a foreign concept. Regardless of our material well-being, as addicts we had little, if any, gratitude. And when we first were told of the need to create a gratitude list, we resisted the idea.

When someone is close to relapse he's usually caught up in what we call "stinkin' thinkin'." These are negative thoughts that tell you that you're not good enough, that you don't have enough, and that you do not do enough. Those nagging self-accusations could be a mantra for most men. If all our thoughts are prayers, too often these are the words we pray regularly, and our attempts to silence them and prove them wrong are rooted in trying to prove our manliness. Their underlying message is this simple phrase: something is missing.

Part of our culture's message about what it means to be masculine is that who we are, in and of ourselves, is not enough. Even as young boys we begin to take in messages from our culture that tell us we're not good enough, that we have to prove our worth. How? By earning a lot of money, by acquiring material things—hot cars, big houses, expensive electronics. By working constantly. By showing off. By being tough. It's all part of a huge attempt to prove to our partners, bosses, relatives, friends, and others that we are worthwhile. As men, we are taught to constantly strive to be better and to get more. Commercials assail us with messages that tell us we'll not be happy until we get this or that. These messages can affect how we feel about ourselves as a man. They tell us that our sense of self-worth is based on people and things—on what's outside ourselves. The result: too many men search throughout their lives to find what's missing when they already have everything they need within.

Most suffering in life stems from this seemingly endless unfulfilled want. Gratitude is the absence of want. It says that you have what you need and you are thankful for everything you have. You are good enough, you have enough, and you are doing enough. Gratitude is living in abundance; in other words, understanding and fully accepting that whatever you have today *is* enough, is perfect, no matter what's missing (you can always find something missing). When you focus on gratitude, you begin to see that in this moment you have everything you need.

Gratitude is the discipline that led me at some point in my sobriety to say, "My name is Dan, and I am a grateful recovering alcoholic." There may even come a time when you find yourself beginning to be grateful for the pain that you have had in your life because that's what led you to become the man you are today. You can literally be grateful for everything. Chris said:

My past is a beautiful thing. All the crying, yelling, doors slamming, pain, joy, fear, laughs, growing up in an alcoholic household, and so on . . . All of it is in the story of my life.

That kind of gratitude can transform your life.

Meditation

> *Meditation is discovering the value*
> *in being quiet and listening and knowing*
> *that as a man I do not have to have*
> *all of the answers.*
>
> – ANDY –

Meditation is the second tool you can use to improve your conscious contact. Step Eleven includes meditation as well as prayer for a reason. If you focus only on prayer, your conscious contact will be limited to talking to your Higher Power; with meditation we learn how to listen.

Prayer tends to be easy for men once we commit to the Twelve Steps. Not a surprise—many of us find it easier to talk than to listen. If you have all the answers, why bother listening to what others have to say? But what kind of relationships would you have if all you ever did was talk? How can you get to know someone if you're the only one talking? Whether you see conscious contact as listening to your Higher Power or to life around you, something quite profound can occur when you take the time to listen—to meditate.

Men in recovery often talk about how they pray in their cars, in the bathrooms where they work, while running, and at many other times during the day. Prayer for many of us has become a natural and integral part of our recovery. Ask us about meditation and how we have incorporated that practice into our lives, however, and many of us will respond by saying that we have tried meditation and could not "stop thinking," so we gave up. Or we may say that we never gave meditation much thought.

However, several of the men I interviewed spoke about having a regular, often daily, meditation practice. Sometimes to begin the day and sometimes to end the night. Sometimes just to be still and listen wherever they are. All the men who practiced meditation talked about the calming and centering effects it had on their lives.

Don't Just Do Something, Sit There

Like prayer, meditation is a simple tool available to us at all times.

If you want to give meditation a quick try, just put this book down right now and try the following: Sit quietly with your back straight and body relaxed. Close your eyes and just pay attention to your breath. Close your mouth and lightly touch your tongue to the back of your front teeth. Slowly breathe in through your nose then breathe out slowly through your nose. Breathe from your diaphragm so you can feel it moving up and down just above your stomach. Notice your thoughts. Try not to focus on them, but instead, just let them go by like clouds passing across the sky. When you do find yourself focusing on your thoughts just calmly return to your breath. It will take practice to simply return to your breath without judging yourself or thinking that you're doing it wrong. Don't judge, just return to noticing your breathing. Remember, too, that simply taking time to sit and be quiet in and of itself is a good thing.

When first trying meditation, many of us believe the goal is to stop thinking. When you first notice all the thoughts in your head, it might be scary. Many of us still have shame about the negative thoughts we have because we believe that they define us or show who we really are. Brandon said that what he appreciates about meditation is "the reminder that my thoughts don't always reflect reality." Moving from your thoughts and returning to your breath is one of the best ways for you to let your thoughts simply be thoughts.

As you continue to meditate and become more aware of all the thoughts running through your head, you might think that meditating should turn off that noise—that if you meditate correctly, you'll stop thinking. Here's the catch: you can't use willpower to stop your thoughts. The more you try to control your thinking, the more insistent your thoughts will be. But you can stop focusing on them. In the meditation technique described above, you are aware of your thoughts passing across your mind, but you calmly keep returning your focus to your breath. Meditation is not about controlling your thinking; it's about letting go of thinking. This is difficult to understand and to do. As men, we're used to taking control and using our minds to think our way out of our problems. Charlie said, "I would never pray or search outside of 'thinking' for guidance." Through the practice of meditation, you can learn a new and effective way to approach life. Meditation helps us learn to live in the present moment. Meditation is a constant process of surrender: surrender to the breath and to the present moment, and letting go of the chaos inside you.

As you practice meditation, whether it's following your breath or focusing on a positive image, word, or saying, you'll get better at it and your thoughts will slow down. Life will slow down. If you've spent your whole life relying on your thinking to get through life, changing this approach won't happen instantly. But you will change, slowly, over the coming days, weeks, months, and years. You can't make meditation work; you let it work. The first step is to admit that you are addicted to the chaos in your mind and that it's been part of the reason your life has been unmanageable! The second step is coming to believe that meditation will make a difference in your life and help restore you to sanity. The third step? Meditate.

Enjoy the Silence

Many men recoil from meditation without really knowing why. Perhaps we find it difficult to be still and quiet. We often would rather be active, in motion, doing things. We may even feel a little guilty if we are not doing something, having been taught that the more we accomplish the better we are and the more we can have. As Larry said:

The practice of spirituality is difficult for so many men because we define ourselves by what we do. In the practice of spirituality, particularly meditation, we see ourselves for who we are being.

Who are you when you do nothing? Who appears in the silence?

Meditation is a deeply personal practice. To simply sit and let you—all of you—arise in the moment without judgment is a very intimate experience. And as we discussed in Step Five, a lot of us feel uncomfortable being close to ourselves. Don't fool yourself: each moment of your life is a moment with yourself. So the question is, how will you experience that intimacy? Few of us learned how to be alone and enjoy the experience, often associating being alone with being lonely. We never knew we could learn how to find joy and satisfaction in just being with ourselves. If you can't stand your own company, how can you expect someone else to? There's no greater intimacy than learning how to be with, accept, and love all of you. That is a gift of meditation.

Keep It Simple

No saying is more identified with the Twelve Step culture than "One day at a time." This is a simple, yet very powerful statement about the present moment. In early recovery, newcomers, who often want to fix everything immediately, are told to take it one hour at a time or even one minute at a time. That is the Twelve Step community teaching you, in a sense, to meditate. All life comes down to one breath at a time, even though we rarely notice it operating at this fundamental level. Meditation can help you slow down enough to begin to see this.

We actually meditate more than we realize. Sitting alone on a dock or in a boat, in the quiet of the morning or evening, waiting for a fish to strike, gardening, or taking a leisurely walk can be quite meditative. Your body and mind slow down, and you feel your connection to all that's around you. You're in the present and at peace. Meditation is something each one of us works out in his own way as we seek to open the channel between ourselves and God as we understand Him. When meditation is a discipline in our life, the world's hectic pace affects us less and less over time. We simply live our lives—one day at a time, one breath at a time.

Be Still and Know That I Am

I was in a meeting many years ago, and I heard a man recite a poem. I have never forgotten the first few lines:

I sought my soul
But my soul I could not see
I sought my God
But my God eluded me
I sought my brother
And I found all three
—Unknown source[4]

Meditation and prayer are the tools the community gives us so that we can learn to take care of our relationships and ourselves to keep in balance. Meditation and prayer allow us to continue to live in community—connected to each other and the mystery of life yet grounded in the confidence of knowing who we are.

The pain of your life comes from the part of you that's grown accustomed to holding on to negative experiences and emotions and that believes something is wrong with you; that all is not well. The degree to which you are at peace with the world depends on the degree to which you are at peace with yourself. Step Eleven allows you to find peace within yourself and peace within this world.

STEP TWELVE

*Having had a spiritual awakening as the result of these steps,
we tried to carry this message to alcoholics, and to practice
these principles in all our affairs.*

**I think as I continue to be of service,
that giving away in our program is so
powerful because there's redemption
in that. It's the phoenix factor—
up from the ashes and being of
service and helping others.**

– JUAN –

Faith without Works Is Dead

Step Twelve says now that you have sobriety and are a new man, share what you have found generously with the world, especially with those who are still suffering from addiction. Lest we become too mesmerized with Step Eleven, we are told that what lies ahead in Step Twelve is "action and more action." Some of us might misunderstand the message in Step Eleven and think that all we have to do is pray for sobriety and it will happen—cultivate our relationship with

God, pray, and the world will unfold before us. But recovery offers no free rides.

Step Eleven, on its own, is powerful. It shows us a path for our growth as a person and for greater connection with our Higher Power and our fellows. Step Eleven, coupled with the mission and action of Step Twelve, is truly transformative—not just for you, but for everyone your life touches. A core concept of Step Twelve is service. Dave was talking about this when he said:

My life and experience exist for the benefit of others. This clashes with the idea I have about "real" men who go through life without extending themselves to others.

This Step now gives us the opportunity to transform ourselves from men of selfishness and self-centeredness to men of service.

To be a man of service is one of the greatest ways we can express our true masculinity. The Twelve Step philosophy is clear: only by "giving it away" can we keep our sobriety. As the Big Book says, "Practical experience shows that nothing will so much insure immunity from drinking as intensive work with other alcoholics."[1] Many of us only sought to be of service to other addicts because our sponsors told us to or because we had been told that we needed to focus on someone else and his problems to put our own life in perspective. We didn't understand at all that in serving others we save ourselves. Every man I spoke with in writing this book said that nothing changed him during his recovery as much as the idea of being focused on others and giving of himself for the benefit of others. As Charlie said, "Giving the gift back to others still in need is my mission as a man."

Like so many other suggested practices, you try being of service and it works; you begin to become the man you always wanted to be. You, too, will see that through service you are claiming your place in the human family. You get to belong again. You change from a man who was only concerned about his own welfare into one who is concerned about the welfare of others. You reach deep down into your humanity and find what is most beautiful about being a man; you get to find what is most beautiful about being you. The best way to keep the gains of recovery is to be a man of service to those you love and to the community.

Our Real Purpose

As discussed earlier, the Big Book states that "our real purpose is to fit ourselves to be of maximum service to God and the people about us."[2] Serving your addiction meant being enslaved by the insatiable obsession and craving. You would do anything for your addiction no matter the negative outcomes or sacrifices. Think back. How much joy did you really get by constantly trying to manipulate situations for your benefit? How much energy did it take to constantly do so? How much pain did you feel when thinking that every situation was supposed to meet your emotional needs? Now you have begun a new kind of service. How do you serve God and others? Where do you fit into the picture? How do you meet others' needs and take care of yourself as well? "Fitting yourself to be of maximum service" requires that you think about how your actions can be for a purpose greater than your needs and interests.

Miguel's story shows how a man can change through his recovery. In his eighth year of sobriety, Miguel's mother-in-law was diagnosed with pancreatic cancer, which decimated her quickly. A group of us watched Miguel's transformation. It was subtle and beautiful. He had one mission: to be with his mother-in-law in her pain and to comfort her in the face of her imminent death. This was the same man who, eight years earlier, was never to be found for any family event because he was too busy getting hammered. To us, the most amazing part of the process was to witness Miguel's humility. He didn't feel he was special; in fact, he often felt as though he was not doing enough.

Some people might be tempted to say, "Big deal! So a selfish drunk changes his life and does what he is supposed to do." Fair enough. I know many wonderful men like Miguel who have discovered this secret to happiness without having an addiction problem. Surely recovery from addiction is not the only path to enlightenment. Many different paths still meet at the top of the mountain. Those of us in recovery are not entitled to applause and congratulation for living a normal life. Nevertheless, we recognize the challenges of the journey and what we had to do to get where we are. For us, the transformation *is* a big deal. We get to rejoin the human race.

We learn to give and that the boundaries of generosity

are endless. We neither ask for nor expect anything in return for our efforts. As a result of our constant efforts to practice these principles, we become workers among workers, family members among family members, and men among men. Mike M. talked about this when he said, "Today, I'm simply a man in his community—rather than someone who is trying to be at the top of the heap or buried underneath."

Sponsorship

> *What I appreciated most about working with my sponsor was that he showed me unconditional love. He showed me that my sexuality has nothing to do with my ability to get sober and whether or not I am worthy of recovery.*
>
> – MIKE M. –

Probably no relationship is more important for men in the Twelve Step culture than the one we have with our sponsors—not just to model recovery but to model what it means to be a man. In my interview with Mike M., he talked about how important it was for him to have a straight man as a sponsor because of the lie inside him that said all straight men would reject him if he told them he was gay. His sponsor had a great response:

> *So! Dude—we're not boyfriends! That has nothing to do with our relationship . . . My responsibility as your sponsor is to show you how to work the Steps.*

The primary purpose of working the Twelfth Step and carrying the message transcends other aspects of who we are.

People come into the rooms of recovery broken, confused, and scared. Their eyes are still clearing from the haze of addiction. Recovery seems like a remote possibility, and often it is a last chance to live—to want to live. We reluctantly grab the lifeline that is thrown to us. Many newcomers are looking for a quick fix to stop the incredible suffering they are experiencing. They are not really interested in a design for living. They are lost in their personas and have no idea where they end and the real parts begin. And then . . . they find a sponsor.

As a sponsor you can teach them how to be adult men in recovery. A man's sponsor is not just a guide through the Steps, he is that man's example of how one can find peace by being sober and knowing who he is. As a man who has found his calling by working in the field of addiction and mental health, Joe P. talked about the role that his Higher Power played in connecting him to his sponsor:

Most of my childhood role models were African American. When you see that two percent of psychiatrists in this country are African American, and then for me to get an African American psychiatrist and a sponsor, wow!

You don't have to be perfect to be a sponsor; you are simply another addict trying to stay sober. You teach by showing other men how to be of service, taking them through the Twelve Steps, and loving them when they cannot love themselves. We can learn something about how to be in relationships by being in a healthy one with our sponsors. Joe H. talked about the role his sponsor has played in helping him share feelings with other men:

He has been a giant part of my ability to discuss my feelings with another man. It was just not comfortable for me to do with anybody, let alone another man.

Sponsors teach us how to have healthy boundaries and to respect ourselves in our relationships.

Sponsorship is the journey to the cliff with another man. As men we often buy into the myth that says we have to make that journey alone. When someone first starts working with his sponsor, his biggest question may be: can I trust him? Casey talked about this:

To go up to some man and ask him to be my sponsor was a huge deal. Quite frankly, it was terrifying. Just the act itself implied weakness and vulnerability. I was admitting that I needed a guide to help me through the Steps because I couldn't do them alone.

A sponsor is essentially saying, "I know a path up the mountain. Trust me." You are hurting and afraid, and have been beaten down. So, with all the humility you can muster, you take the risk. Step by Step you follow him. He points out all the places where you might stumble—where he stumbled. Each day you have an opportunity to reach out to your sponsor for direction, support, a loving butt-kicking, and any other guidance he can provide. With each Step you take, you trust him more, and you begin to see that your sponsor is teaching you how to be in a relationship.

The intimacy and vulnerability a man experiences with

his sponsor can at first be more intense and genuine than what he's felt with his family and partner. Your relationship with your sponsor is a kind of test showing you whether you can be in an honest relationship with another person. And you can!

Nothing requires more honesty than Step Five and so nothing should be treated with more reverence and sense of privilege than hearing another person's Fifth Step. Many people do their Fifth Step with their sponsors, and it can be the turning point for the sponsor-sponsee relationship. You have the opportunity to learn what it means to be open and honest about who you are, to be loved, and to be accepted. You can then carry that honesty and openness with you into all of your relationships.

Bill was my first sponsor and the first man to teach me about being a man in recovery. I yearned for a connection with another man, an older man. I, like so many broken young men coming into recovery, was looking for a father. I had given up on my own dad because I thought he had chosen the bottle over me. Bill watched me come into that meeting room and saw how scared I was. He saw that I was lost and had no idea how to be sober. Bill stepped in because he saw how desperately I needed someone to love me.

It was a very simple gesture that started our relationship. We went for a walk. A walk, though, that changed my life. He asked me questions about my life. He looked me in the eye and was gentle in the way he spoke to me. There was no judgment. He cared about me for no reason other than the fact that I was another suffering alcoholic. He knew I was hurting, and he wanted to help me feel better. He knew I couldn't love myself, so he stepped in to love me until I could. He modeled—and continues to do so to this day—how a man can be strong, confident, gentle, vulnerable, compassionate, loving, funny, caring, firm, honest, open, disciplined, and accountable. He went from being a father figure to becoming the man I consider to be my father today. I strive to pass what I learned from him on to the men I sponsor, as best I can, and to help them achieve the emotional sobriety that Bill nurtured in me.

All Our Affairs

We've talked about emotional sobriety as the result of our efforts to grow up. You are responsible for knowing and expressing how you feel and for the impact you have in all your relationships. Emotional sobriety does not only apply to how you interact with others. How you care for yourself, too, is an essential part of cultivating emotional sobriety. In practicing these principles in all our affairs, we begin to see that the concept of self-care is broader and deeper than we realized. It can include paying attention to your physical health, eating well, exercising, accepting the need for medication as a recovery support when our mental health requires it, attending personal counseling and couples counseling, and doing intimate and intensive work with other men. These areas are critical to how we care for ourselves and our emotional sobriety.

Paying Attention to Your Physical Health

Recovery includes healing your mind, spirit, and body. While we are quite good at emphasizing the mind and the spirit in the Twelve Step community, we don't always emphasize taking care of our bodies. Recovery is about achieving balance in our lives. If mind, body, and spirit represent a three-legged stool, when one of those legs is broken, the stool will not stand.

It's likely that you never noticed the huge toll your addiction was taking on your body. Addiction destroys our will to live, so doctors become the enemy. In the throes of our addiction, we were afraid doctors would take away our drugs and we were afraid they would tell us what we, at some level, already knew—that we were sick and needed help.

Once we are in recovery our attitude toward our health can and should change. We have revived our will to live. We go to see doctors because we notice the damage our body has sustained and how our body is reacting to being without drugs. Now that the poisons are out of our system, we want to feel as good as we can. We listen to our bodies. We do everything we can to take care of our bodies because now we care what happens to us.

Eating Well

Chances are while you were active in your addiction you filled your body with all manner of junk food along with all the drugs. The longer you are sober, the more you realize that your body truly is the temple of your soul. As you begin to take better care of yourself, you'll pay more attention to what and how much you eat. You will begin to notice that certain foods seem to be better for you. You will realize that you may or may not like a certain food or the effect it has on you and will choose not to eat it. You will begin to see that nutritious food can actually make you feel good because it's helping your body become healthier and stronger. It's finally getting the nutrients it needs to function normally—and, of course, the drugs are gone. Dan J. said, "In the last year I changed my diet, and that change relieved some stomach issues that were caused by poor diet and stress." Because you now truly care about yourself, you'll understand that the food you eat is more than just fuel to keep you alive—it's the energy that feeds your spirit.

Exercise

Now that you are in recovery, you also see and feel your body again, and that may be a shock. You're probably out of shape, over- or underweight, and even ill. You may be embarrassed about how you look. You may feel as though you don't have the time or the energy to exercise. You may even, at some level, think you don't deserve to feel healthy and strong because of how much you abused your body. Like everything in recovery, the only way you can change is to take the necessary action. Without a regular form of exercise in your life, your recovery will suffer. Now that you're eating better, you should have the energy. You need to begin exercising your body. Regular exercise will help restore your emotional balance, give you even more energy, and help you regain a healthy metabolism. If you persevere, you soon feel better about yourself and your body, and your body will thank you. Exercise is self-reinforcing: the more you do, the better and stronger you'll feel, and the more you'll be excited to continue.

Paying Attention to Your Mental Health

When it comes to recognizing mental health issues in recovery, there are three kinds of men in the Twelve Step community: men who do not have mental health issues, men who have them and don't think or realize that they do, and men who recognize their problems and get treatment for them. Research shows that 60–70 percent of men in recovery have a diagnosable mental health issue,[3] and the Twelve Step community has historically given them little support.

Medication

In the past ten years, however, the community has become increasingly more accepting of and informed about mental health issues. Unfortunately, too many in recovery still believe that using medications is unnecessary or an indication of not working the program. Brian, now a child psychiatrist, talked about his experience:

Early in recovery, I was hospitalized in a psychiatric facility and treated for depression with medication. I also regularly attended AA meetings. There is no question in my mind that psychiatric treatment was critical to my recovery because I had experienced depression severe enough to place me at serious risk of suicide. I did not run into any opposition to medication until I got a sponsor who challenged me to reconsider my position on the issue. I believe today that was an abuse of sponsorship. I also believe strongly what is stated in AA-approved literature on medication, that "No AA plays doctor." Over the years, I have been on and off medication, mainly antidepressant medication. My feeling is that the decision to take meds should be left to the professionals who prescribe them and that we need to be honest with our doctors and follow their directions.

More than half of the men I interviewed had either been on medication for their mental health issues at some point in their recovery or were still taking medication. Several of them talked about the internal process they had to go through to accept their need for medical help. Juan, who is in long-term recovery, recently got on medication and had a very positive response from his family and from others close to him in recovery:

Dealing with this was a long process. It began with talking about this with others—my wife, sponsor, friends, family—who have had experience with it. Then came a formal admitting to self and seeking help.

Many men are so used to living in anxiety, depression, anger, and general moodiness that they think that's normal. Sadly, because these men are miserable, they make the lives of those around them unnecessarily miserable, too. Too often we think that some degree of suffering must accompany sobriety. Too many of us have become so accustomed to seeing suffering as a part of life that we wear our unaddressed issues like medals of honor. The best you can do for any man, including yourself, who has questions about mental health issues is to help him find capable and knowledgeable professional help. If you do not try medication, you will never know if it can help you. If the medication does not make a difference, that's valuable information for you. If the medication does make a difference, then you and those closest to you will experience the benefits.

Counseling

Whether it's individual, family, or couples counseling, the right counselor at the right time in your recovery can be a godsend. The Big Book says:

> *God has abundantly supplied this world with fine doctors, psychologists, and practitioners of various kinds. Do not hesitate to take your health problems to such persons . . . Their services are often indispensable in treating a newcomer and in following his case afterward.[4]*

Every man I interviewed for this book had some individual counseling in his recovery. Contrary to the stereotype about men being unwilling to ask for help, many of these men have not only been to couples counseling, but they initiated it! Dan J.'s experience is similar to that of many of the men:

> *I have had experience with individual, marriage, and anger management counseling. All three were initiated by me or my wife and me.*

A partner who's not willing to go to counseling should not stop you from doing so. There should be no stigma about seeing a counselor. Every married couple, especially those affected by addiction, should have whatever support they feel they need. If you think that working with a professional will help your recovery and your relationships, by all means talk to other men, find a good one, and make an appointment.

Counseling and therapy can offer tremendous support

both for you and for others in your life. Jo was clear that more than ten years of counseling—both individual and couples— were essential to helping him learn how to have true intimacy in his closest relationships. Do what you can to encourage the men you know to pursue whatever support they need, and honor them for their courage.

Men's Work

As men, it is a good idea to do some of our healing work with other men. Charlie said, "I believe that men must have as a part of our recovery at least one circle of only our sex where we can learn to love the unique and beautiful powers of being men."

Men's groups can be a wonderful additional support to help you look at any or all areas of your life. They differ from Twelve Step meetings or work with your sponsor in that they're not structured in the same way and they're not focused solely on the Twelve Steps. A men's group can offer you a wonderful and unique opportunity to talk with other men openly about a range of issues—for example, problems with anger, sex, relationships, homophobia, confusion about being a man, past hurts, and whatever else you and the group choose to explore. Some men in the Twelve Step community hold retreats or create outside groups to do this additional work. These groups have the added benefit of the common language of the Steps to guide their work. You can do men's work many ways, but choose carefully. Not all groups are the same. Interviewing a few will help you get a feel for them and find one that best fits your needs.

Loving Yourself

> *Really what it comes down to with all*
> *these things . . . is that I love myself*
> *no matter what is going on.*
>
> —CHRIS

> *But obviously you cannot transmit*
> *something you haven't got.*
>
> —BIG BOOK[5]

We hear over and over again in recovery that we cannot transmit something we do not have. How can you love another person if you don't love yourself? Reggie said:

Prior to recovery I was a bitter person who acted out of his self-loathing and lack of confidence. I was incapable of seeing others as they were when I was so focused on my self-centered fears.

Most addicted men struggle with deep self-loathing. Here's the deal: if you can't learn to respect and love yourself, at least to some degree, you will not stay sober. And Brian added:

People who do not love themselves hold others hostage in relationships and have a hard time trusting enough to allow others to be independent and grow. Working the Steps of the program is all about self-love.

So what does it mean to love yourself? After five years of sobriety, I still found myself miserable and wondering how I was ever going to get out of my spiritual misery. The answer was quite simple. I learned that my relationship with myself should be as important as any other relationships I have. Randy, my first counselor, put it this way:

Can you imagine if you treated any of your friends the way you treat yourself? You'd be arrested!

Your relationship with yourself, like every other relationship, is one that you have to pay attention to and nurture, and for which you have to be accountable. Chris talked about this:

When I say "love" I mean happy. Am I happy with myself and my life? To me true happiness comes when I can say I love who I am, what I'm doing, where I'm at, when I'm doing it.

Loving yourself is different from self-centered behavior. Truly loving yourself allows you to love and be of service to others and connect to the world around you, too. If you're only focused on you and your need, it's not self-love—it's selfishness.

My friend, Paul, with nine years of sobriety, crystallized this concept for me. He talked about the challenges he had taking care of himself in sobriety. He talked about the fear he had as a man because it meant he had to learn how to put his needs first in a healthy way. Many of us weren't raised to take care of ourselves physically, let alone emotionally. Too often we became very dependent on our mothers and other women, leaving us lacking confidence in our ability to take care of ourselves. Our fathers and other men often did the opposite, leaving us to fend for ourselves.

The concept of self-love is not anything new. Too often, though, it simply gets lost in our society—one filled with fears of codependency and with sexism and homophobia. We suffer, and we cause others to suffer, because of our fear and ignorance.

Earl, a man with decades of recovery, spoke in our men's recovery meeting one day about the importance of men learning how to love themselves and, even more, to see all the times that reflect our struggles to love ourselves. I watched as he sat calmly in his chair with his back hunched ever so slightly looking another man right in the eye, and he spoke as matter-of-factly about the need for that man to learn how to love himself as if he were recounting the scores from the baseball game the night before. He then told that man how much he cared about him. Everyone listened. Nobody laughed at him. That shows the power of recovery to transform men and how the community teaches a man to love himself.

A Fellowship of the Spirit

The fellowship you can find in the Twelve Step community is nothing short of magical. You can meet, share with, and learn from men from all walks of life. Kerry provided a wonderful example of the magic:

> I was at an AA convention, and this big brute who fit your stereotype of a whisky-drinking redneck got up and started talking about the chicks he would date and his Harley trips with his drinkin' buds. I was about to leave, and then he mentioned his gay son. He told the story of his son contracting AIDS and dying. The most precious time in his life was getting into bed with his son as he passed away. This was a moment he would have missed if he had been an active alcoholic, just as I would have missed witnessing what real men get to do in recovery. We get to be who we really are. I had quickly dismissed someone who had an important gift for me.

We are creating connections and relationships with other men that absolutely defy the types of relationships our society tells us we can—or should—have. We have been exposed to the pain and disappointment of living in the world of "self-will run riot." We have a fellowship of the spirit that transcends the superficial and false labels we take on in our day-to-day life. This fellowship is based on the belief that we are all more alike than not.

In the fellowship of the spirit we don't care what you do for a living or what you look like. We do not care about who you were. What is more important is the type of man you are and how you live. We do not care who you love—only that you do it well. We are trying to undo years, even decades, of habits and ways of interacting with ourselves and with others. Much that we were taught harmed us. We are learning how to be more healthy and alive. It is a bumpy road, and we inevitably make mistakes and act in ways that are not who we wish to be. So we learn from our mistakes and continue the journey together in the spirit of forgiveness and growth.

In Twelve Step meetings you'll often hear someone say to a newcomer, "We are going to love you until you are able to love yourself." As you grow in your recovery and deepen your relationship with your Higher Power, you learn to love yourself. You'll recognize that you are part of the human community. With the confidence that this brings, you'll be able to give back to that community by helping those who still suffer. You will be a role model for other men coming into the recovery community and pass on to them the Big Book's promise and invitation:

> *Life will take on new meaning. To watch people recover, to see them help others, to watch loneliness vanish, to see a fellowship grow up about you, to have a host of friends—this is an experience you must not miss.*[6]

MEN AND GRIEF

Grief, and the ability for men
to experience and work through grief,
is the foundation of the work
we do in recovery.

—ANDY

"If the only work you did with men was to teach them to grieve, it would be enough." I heard these words when I was attending a weekend retreat for men. Sometimes we can see men's grief and sometimes we can't; sometimes we can see our own grief, but most of the time we cannot. What we very often see are the hardened faces of men who have trained themselves to not cry in order to seem tough, men who have swallowed the pain that they have experienced throughout their lives. We will see the men who have been strong for everyone else during the losses of their lives. We will see the anger, sarcasm, and depression that suffocate men. The grief is under the façade, and it does not take much to touch it.

Men's grief is the sadness, hurt, and loss that we have stuffed deep down inside ourselves and that we pretend does not exist. Our grief is the pain we carry about the numerous

losses we have experienced in our lives and never let ourselves feel. We carry pain from the traumas that continue
to haunt us. We have learned to ignore grief, but it does not
ignore us. Juan talked about how disconnected from grief he
was before recovery:

> *What was typical of my experience with grief was a significantly
> delayed process. I would freeze it, lock it down, and not feel
> anything . . . until months later, when I'd be hit with a wave of
> emotion.*

In working through our grief we find the gateway to wholeness as human beings. What we find at the bottom of the well
of grief are the profound awakenings and peace that grow out
of the work we do. As Charlie said, "Today I welcome grieving
as a form of praise for what I'm losing and have lost."

Grief in Recovery

Most of us come into recovery with some degree of grief
eating at us. When we first get sober, our feelings can be so
raw that we can be surprised—even embarrassed—to find
ourselves crying in group sessions or while at a meeting. Yet
most of us who went through treatment did not learn how
to grieve. We may have been given a pamphlet, told to see
a grief counselor, or even been referred to a grief group, but
too often that work is ineffective and we remain stuck. If we
do not learn anything about grief in treatment, will the men
of the Twelve Step community teach us how to grieve?

Grief work starts in Step One. We grieve the loss of a
substance that has been our best friend, our lover, our con-

fidant, our God. It continues in Steps Four and Step Five. As we begin to see ourselves more clearly, we grieve the loss of that part of our lives connected to our addiction. In Steps Eight and Nine, we grieve the pain we have caused others and ourselves—grief that we may not know how to handle. When talking with Juan about Step Eight, he became very emotional, even tearing up, as he recounted some of his past behavior, regretting that he would never be able to find someone he'd harmed. Though his actions occurred more than twenty years ago, Juan still grieves the person he became in his addiction and the pain he caused another.

Our sobriety opens us to our emotional life. In recovery, we are given the gift of experiencing our pain in the moment. Joe H. talked about his experience with his father's death:

My father died just five months after I first sobered up. I was amazed that I was able to feel my grief. I talked to my spouse, to others, and listened to music that triggered my grief. I fully felt it, and that allowed me to have peace with my father's passing.

Because he was no longer numbing himself with drugs, Joe H. was able to experience the full impact of his love for his father and the loss caused by his death. Joe H. let himself grieve because he was now part of a culture that encouraged him to do so.

As we stay sober, life continues. Opportunities for grief will come. Quinn talked about the death of his spouse of thirty-three years:

She supported my sobriety and was proud of me for facing this issue. My sober years allowed me to bring more of myself to the relationship. I miss her.

I watched Quinn grieve for two years. He would go through a whole array of emotions—anger, gratitude, sadness, despair, loneliness, and joy. He would sit in a meeting and quietly cry, saying how he knew the circle of men he was with was a safe place for him to grieve.

Andy, who has been in Al-Anon for more than twenty-years, felt a great loss that came when he finally admitted his powerlessness and his illusions of self-control. He grieved the abuse he suffered from his father as a child and how that abuse had leaked into his own family. Andy said, "Grief, and the ability for men to experience and work through grief, is the foundation of the work that men do in recovery."

Here are examples of just some of the experiences that we have to grieve in recovery:

- *Deaths of loved ones*
- *Deaths of children*
- *Ending of significant relationships*
- *Violence that has been perpetrated on us*
- *Violence that we have perpetrated on others*
- *The loss of our addictive substances*
- *The way that we are raised as men*
- *For veterans of war, the actions taken as part of that process*
- *Any number of actions we took while active in our addiction that violated our values or hurt people*
- *Miscarriages, aborted pregnancies (particularly those in which we were given no say)*
- *Our loss of childhood*

• *Loss of jobs*

• *Moving; loss of home and place*

Look at the items on this list and if even one of them applies to you, you probably have grief work to do. The more items on the list that apply to your life experience, the more important it is for you to get support as you look at your grief. Talk to your sponsor and to the old-timers you know. Ask them how they deal with grief. Write in a journal. Read books about grief. Bring the subject up in your meetings. Get professional help and support. Join a grief group. Use your meditation and prayer time. You won't have to worry about getting in touch with your grief; your grief will get in touch with you. The hope, though, is that you will listen. When grief comes to men, too many of us try to ignore it, even while it eats away at our physical and mental health as it tries to get our attention. Pay attention. Listen.

Big Boys Do *Cry*

Grief is not just about crying. Grief is a range of emotions connected to the process of letting go of the pain of loss. Our society does not recognize men's grief. In fact, we have a hard time recognizing grief in general. The idea that men who cry are somehow weak is so deeply embedded in our culture's collective psyche that most men and women do not know how to respond to men's grief. Men's grief is about our wholeness, our freedom. Juan talked about losing his trusted companion, a Rottweiler, from his early sobriety:

He was so pivotal in my recovery . . . When he died there was an instant feeling of loss and sadness, and I was able to weep and feel that loss, connect to that loss, and also feel gratitude for his existence.

You might be asking right now, "Okay, so how do I do this grief work?" First and foremost, you have to learn how to embrace that part of you that is sad and hurting. Start with the very basics. Allow yourself to have those feelings. Learn to not swallow your grief. Try to not hide it behind clenched jaws, sarcastic remarks, or by choking back your tears. And remember, just talking about grief is only a part of working through grief.

For many men, getting in touch with our grief is the last experience we want to have. We are not able to cry—we have literally forgotten how. Some of us are afraid that if we start crying, we may never stop. We have spent so much time being strong, keeping it together, and stuffing our feelings. We don't want anyone to think we are sad or hurting because we still have not accepted these feelings ourselves.

As you consciously allow grief into your life, it may arise in some very interesting or unexpected ways. Try to be open. Let the sadness come up as it needs to. Welcome your sadness without judgment. Trust the process. When you allow yourself to grieve, you open the door to the painful experiences you have carried with you, perhaps even since your childhood. Juan talked about how he now experiences grief in recovery:

For so many years, I didn't want to feel those emotions that I saw as negative, unattractive—as unmanly emotions . . . Tears were weak . . . You did not cry. The gift I've received in recovery is that I can weep. I remember the tears prerecovery were unconnected.

I was never really sure what they were connected to. Today, there's very solid connection.

Your Higher Power will show you the path. Be open to it because the path may not look as you expect. Express your willingness and thank your Higher Power for the strength and guidance to do this work. The rest will take care of itself.

The River of Grief

Grief is like a river moving through the landscape of our lives. At three years sober, two years after my father's death, I was at a meeting. Another man and I had just talked about the embarrassment we felt about crying. Wanda, a former stripper from Kansas City and one of my adopted grandmas, looked at me and said, "There is nothing wrong with crying. It is just taking a shower on the inside." As I was leaving the meeting a friend of mine, a big ex-football player turned nurse named Mark, came up to me, smiled at me with nothing but love in his eyes, and hugged me. I hugged him back, and as I did the tears started. Then the sobbing. I had not cried since the day of my father's funeral. I felt as if something inside me was trying to claw its way out. I ended up having a panic attack, barely able to breathe, because I was fighting it so much. My grief had gotten in touch with me. Sometimes the river of grief is so narrow you can jump across it easily, and other times, it is the mighty Mississippi that will drown you if you do not honor it.

I have cried often since then. It's happened while doing men's work in a group, when I have broken through the shame of certain behavior, and in the safety of being with my partner. I am still learning to give myself permission to cry, especially when I am alone. I am learning from my sponsor, the men in the community, like Quinn, and through the examples of the men whom I sponsor.

One day at a time, the community of men will teach you and invite you to become more whole by admitting, accepting, and releasing your grief. Miguel talked about an experience he had with another man that illustrates this point beautifully:

We were checking in at an AA meeting when I noticed that one of my sponsees was across the room in the circle. He had shared with great emotion that his wife had asked him to move out. He was very sad and close to tears. I could feel his pain and grief since I had been in the same situation eight years before. When it came around to me, I told him that I loved him and needed to give him a hug. I held him tight until his tears came. It seemed like a long time to hug a man in front of fifty other men. The room was silent and the moment was powerful.

Sometimes you fight the river. Sometimes you try to run from the river. Sometimes you don't know what the river is going to look like as you turn a corner in the deep canyon of your pain. But sometimes you don't fight it and you don't run from it. Instead, you let the river take you where it will. You simply allow the river to wash over you as if you were the river.

A Poem to Grieve and Honor My Father

I wrote the following poem for my father the day after they found him dead in our family home due to complications from alcoholism at the age of fifty-four. I read it at his funeral later that week. It was published in the holiday newsletter for Father Martin's Ashley House in 1995. I share it here to honor my father, Owen Martin Griffin, son of Edward and Elizabeth, father to Daniel and Jennifer, husband to Sharon.

The world doesn't stop for Death
But it seems to have stopped for me
I lose myself in simple thoughts
Avoiding that old familiar voice whispering
From behind the corner
Wanting me to destroy myself
To avoid the Pain that sits there
Scraping my heart with its claws
And something else, another voice whispers:
"He will not die in Vain."

The call came and opened a chasm in my life
"I don't know how else to tell you . . .
But your father's dead."
Suddenly what was talked about
With strong speech around the tables
Was Real
The final thread had been cut
A din of confusion filled my head
Emptying out as tears
Between every sober breath I took
I heard the voice again:
"He will not die in Vain."

I watched the Sun set
Below the clouds and prayed to God:
"Help me remember the good times."
Like waking in my father's arms
As he carried me from the car
Helping me to draw Frankenstein
Lying next to him while the Eagles
Or the Outlaws or Emmylou played
The jokes, the smiles
The wrestling on the floor and even
The kisses goodnight
Going out to dinner when "The Bridgies" came
A baseball game, or maybe just
"Sleep tight."
The love he showed as best he could
I understand today
And so the voice it comes:
"He will not die in Vain."

The Dragon beat St. George
I watched my father slowly die
I did not understand
What did I do wrong?
Night after night choosing the Bottle
Over me
The fights, the shame, the guilt, the fear
The empty stare of hollow eyes
Hide the insanity behind
A pressed-suit and a silk tie,

A well-manicured lawn, nice cars
Nice house—conjure up a social smile
Don't think when people say "How are you doing?"
They really want to know the truth
Just nod and smile and say "Fine"
As you slowly die inside
And the voice it screams:
"You will not die in Vain."

Some will say you didn't fight
Some you fought too much
Others may think you were weak
Or you used it as a crutch
But nobody questions the cancer
When it takes a life
But to be an alcoholic
Means something isn't right
So let us not pretend or deny
The simple truth—that lies
Tangled up in difficulty
Refusing to come loose
Death is for the living
That we may some day reach
The conclusions that they leave us
And the lessons that they teach.
So for now I say goodbye
Until I see you again
And Promise to live my life
So you will not have died in Vain.

MEN
AND RELATIONSHIPS

All my relationships have improved
in recovery: they are now honest and
reflect the truth of who I am.

- DOMINIQUE -

Once we get sober, the rest of our recovery is about relationships—with our Higher Power, ourselves, and others. All the men I spoke with deeply value their relationships. They have decided to challenge the myths about men and relationships, and to help give other men the tools they need to succeed in all their relationships.

For most of us, learning how to have a meaningful and fulfilling relationship becomes our life's work in recovery. Joe P., who witnessed an incredible amount of violence while growing up, talked about this:

All that trauma and immaturity kept me on the run from rela-
tionships and from myself. In recovery, I've learned how to stay
engaged, to talk about issues, and work them out.

We have the capacity to express ourselves emotionally, get our needs met, and, most important, meet the emotional needs of our partners. Casey said:

Working the Steps has helped me be more open about what's going on with me. I can be a better friend and partner now.

Men in recovery are not afraid to let others know how much we value their love, friendship, and support. We cry when we feel sad and hurt, express joy when we feel the exuberance of life, and express fear or insecurity without worrying that it might make us look weak. Jo talked about going through a divorce and looking for support in his church:

Sharing my pain through that wasn't just important for the congregation, it was crucial for me. I remember breaking down in front of them and crying. I never would have done that before, even earlier in my recovery. To really be whole, I needed to let those feelings out and share them.

We need to allow ourselves to be who we are, not who others think we should be.

Working to improve each of your relationships is a task that will continue throughout your life. Pay attention and be honest with yourself by looking at the whole relationship, especially your part. Yes, some relationships will end, but that happens. It doesn't mean you're not capable of having successful, nurturing relationships.

In this chapter, we'll look at some of the most significant relationships in our lives: those with other men, our fathers, and women.

Men Who Love Men[1]

> *My relationships with other men*
> *have always been about guy stuff—*
> *sports and so on. Not until recovery*
> *have I had the opportunity to talk to*
> *other men on a deeper level.*
>
> – JOE H. –

Our male culture is rife with homophobia that keeps men from being close to one another and yes, from loving one another. Many of us men have felt trapped inside a masculine script that prevents us from connecting with our closest male friends in a meaningful way before we get sober. Miguel talked about his relationships, before and after recovery, with male friends going back to high school, more than twenty years ago:

I really didn't open up and talk about feelings, desires, and other things with my guy friends. It was mostly sports banter and maybe we'd touch upon family in a surface way but no other relationships.

Most men do want to connect with other guys, and we want them to accept us and see us as people worthy of love. And yet we have no idea how to do this. Joe P. mentioned how we often connect with other men through conversations about sports, sex, or work but seldom touch on what's really going on with us or our relationships:

We can huddle up and talk about men's stuff and it makes us feel good. But when it gets to the relationship stuff, I see men back off. Once we learn how to talk to each other about everything, we realize it works, for us and our families.

In Twelve Step communities, men are expected to communicate with each other in a way that is foreign to most of us, especially in our relationships with men. Rob talked about how he experienced this change in relating to other men:

My ideas of manhood said that we should only reveal our emotional side with women, so to be in a meeting and hear men discussing their innermost struggles and weaknesses was a real milestone.

In recovery, we need each other to help save each other's lives. Joe P. said it poignantly:

I thought I was supposed to die from alcoholism like my dad. I couldn't believe that men were getting healthy and getting sober.

All the men acknowledged that they would neither be sober nor the men they are today if not for the many men—most of whom are also in recovery—who supported and loved them. As Casey said:

My relationships with men have changed. The Twelve Steps help us share a common problem and a common solution. You share what's going on with you, you're involved in fellowship, and you share with men outside the meetings. The Twelve Steps have allowed me to have these more open relationships with men.

As a result, men like Casey have learned how to love other men so that the newcomer can find the same freedom that they have found—not only from alcohol and other drugs, but the true freedom promised in the Twelve Steps. In Miguel's words, "My relationships today with other men are of a quality I never achieved in my drinking days."

My voice still shakes a little when I tell some of the men in my life that I love them. A little voice in my head pops up and says, "Don't say it, Dan. Don't do it." It doesn't matter who I say this to, be it Bill, who has been a father to me ever since I first got sober, or my good friend, West, who's been a good friend to me and I to him. We care deeply for one another, and we both want love in our lives. Nevertheless, I still get nervous at the thought of letting him know how much he means to me. Matt, another great friend, and I end a lot of our conversations with one of us telling the other one, "I love you." And why shouldn't we—it is true. Matt and I have been through incredible experiences together, and I would do anything for him. That is love. So, why should I not express this directly to him? Because it is not a manly thing to do? How often do you prevent yourself from telling other men how you feel about them? What gets in the way? Are you willing to do something different?

Here's a wonderful story. I was talking recently to Mike H., who has almost forty years of sobriety and is the CEO of a large chemical dependency treatment business. He said:

I want to share something with you, Dan. The other day I was driving home, listening to my voice mails when I heard this message: "I love you. You do not have to call me back. I just was thinking of you and wanted you to know that I love you." Well, I called the guy back, Dan, and I told him the same thing, "I love you, too." "You didn't have to call me back," he said. "I know and I wanted to let you know that I love you, too." Dan, this guy is the CEO of a huge construction contracting business. He and I are not supposed to be the guys who say that kind of stuff.

Nevertheless, they are and they do. Interactions like this are happening every day all over the world, but sadly, for the most part we keep them secret.

Our Fathers

> *My relationship with my father*
> *unfolded into a shared journey*
> *of love and integrity.*
>
> – CHARLIE –

The imprint of our fathers rests deeply on our souls. We have learned how to be men from them. We have tried to be men like them and not like them. Many of our fathers were not the men who they really wanted to be. In recovery, some of us can break a cycle that has been destroying the hearts and souls of the men in our families for some time. The possibility that your children will know a father who is sober, first of all, and loving, emotionally present, and confident in who he is as a man is one of the greatest gifts you can give to them and to this world.

The men I interviewed had varying degrees of closeness to their fathers. Men like Joe P. had to find peace with their fathers after they had died. Andy, who was severely abused by his father, has not spoken to him since 1981. Other men, like Charlie and Dan J., had suffered some abuse from their fathers but were able to heal and create loving relationships with them. Still other men, like Dave and Rob, had great relationships with their fathers before their addiction that continued into their recovery.

You can use the Steps to help you heal your relationship with your father. Below are some examples of the father work that you can do to continue to grow in your recovery:

- *Do Steps Four and Five with a focus just on your father—and being a father yourself, if this applies.*
- *Work Steps Six and Seven in the context of the defects you accuse your father of having, and then talk to your sponsor, partner, and close friends to see if they see these same defects in you.*
- *Revisit Steps Eight and Nine to see if there are any amends you need to do with your father, your sons, your uncles, your brothers, or other father figures in your life.*
- *Write an uncensored letter to your father—from you as an adult or as a child.*
- *Whether your father is dead or still with us, share your joys and pain with him . . . but without blaming him for your unhappiness or without letting him off the hook for any of his past unacceptable behavior.*

Regardless of the father work you do through the Twelve Steps, the most important goal is always the same: do the work. Whether or not your dad is still alive, I implore you to make peace with him. The key to making peace with yourself as a man lies in making peace with your father, no matter how present he was in your life. The degree to which a man has made peace with his relationship with his father can dramatically affect how he'll be as a partner, lover, sponsor, father, brother, and friend.

Women—Can't Live without Them

I was at a class with my partner Nancy when I heard the saying "Men feel loved when they have sex. Women have sex when they feel loved."

While this is an overgeneralization to which there are many exceptions, these two statements open up some interesting insights into intimacy with women and have profoundly affected the quality of my relationship with Nancy. The emotional and sexual health of a relationship are deeply connected. Ignore either one and you put the relationship at risk.

Men Feel Loved when They Have Sex

It's not unusual for men to place a great deal of importance on sex in general and on their sexual relationship with their partner in particular. Certainly our desire for sex is a basic biological need, but much of how we view sex we learn from the culture in which we're raised. If you're not having sex with your partner, you may think it's because she doesn't love you or find you attractive. Miguel talked about how, while actively alcoholic, his cheating on his partner was due to feeling rejected and unimportant—feelings he was unable to talk about. When Nancy once turned down an overture of mine, I realized that my reaction was about much more than her not wanting to have sex. It triggered a shame response in me that often resulted in anger or feelings of rejection, after which I'd just turn away from her. Until I could communicate those feelings to her, I was stuck repeating the same behavior.

It's so important to talk about such feelings and thoughts with your partners, yet many men know very little about how to create a relationship environment that will help them feel safe enough to do so. Far too many relationships are destroyed because we are unable to talk about what is really going on in our heads and hearts. What would you share with her? What are you afraid to tell her? What are you keeping from your partner because you are stuck trying to be a man?

Women Have Sex when They Feel Loved

If you don't understand that for most women, sex and relationship are closely connected, you will often find yourself feeling like a victim. Far too often we complain about the lack of sex in our lives when we ought to be thinking about our partner. What is her experience in the relationship? How have you been treating her? Does she feel loved and valued by you? Or have you been ignoring her, using pornography, flirting with coworkers—actions that can escalate to full-fledged affairs, sex addiction, or soliciting prostitutes? Such activities separate you from your partner, and she will feel this separation. Do you spend more time taking from your relationship than looking for ways to nourish it? Each day, think about what you are doing to help your partner feel loved. What are you doing to be of service to your partnership? If you were to actually ask that question every day, it could have a wonderfully positive impact on your relationship *and* your sex life.

Recovery will change how you relate to women. Once you realize that you can be open and honest with your partner, you will have a whole new way of relating to all the women in your life. Deep down, many men are actually afraid of women. If that's you, until you face that fear your connections with women will always be tentative—at arm's length. Brandon said this about his relationships with women:

I'm getting better at seeing women for who they are—equals who struggle through life and who have challenges, too. Now that my worthiness doesn't hinge as much on a woman's response, I see them as people, not objects to fill me with purpose or satisfaction.

We often put women on pedestals because society tells us over and over that only they can give us what we desperately want—love. As Dan J. said, "I spent a lot of time in my dating relationships looking for that perfect woman who would make it all better." She does not exist.

Until you realize that a woman will not and cannot complete you, your relationships with women will suffer. If you want a mother, there are probably women who will line up to play that role, but you will sacrifice your chance to have a mature relationship and the happiness and self-respect that brings. If you want an equal partner, you'll have to work for it. It will be the most challenging, scary, exhausting, frustrating, exciting, and fulfilling work you will ever do in your life.

Codependence

> *My sponsor told me that one of the*
> *most important classes I could take*
> *was on codependency. He was right.*
> *Codependency means immaturity—*
> *immaturity caused by*
> *childhood trauma.*

– JOE P. –

Many men do not like to talk about codependency and they may struggle with codependency long into their recovery because they tend to see it as something that women do. What, exactly, is codependency? According to Melody Beattie, who popularized the term in her widely read book *Codependent No More,* "a codependent person is one who has let another person's behavior affect him or her, and who is obsessed with controlling that person's behavior."[2] The key here is the attempt to control.

It may be helpful to understand the difference between interdependent and codependent relationships. In a relationship, each person's behavior affects the other. The closer and more intimate the relationship, the greater the opportunity for your partner's behavior to affect you and vice-versa. In other words, all relationships are interdependent. When you do not take care of yourself and let another person's behavior affect your ability to make healthy decisions, that is codependent behavior. If you are in an intimate relationship and your partner's behavior does not affect you at all, then you may be a robot! An interdependent relationship falls somewhere between these two extremes.

Men who grew up in addicted or chaotic families or who were abused as children will very likely struggle with some degree of codependency. Dan J. talked about his discovery of his codependent behavior:

I thought it only applied to romantic relationships, but my co-dependence can extend to everyone. My loyalty is often codependence in disguise. I have ruined friendships by not allowing them to change from how I perceived them.

Here are just a few of the signs that may indicate you're acting codependently in a relationship: holding resentments, avoiding conflict, gossiping about the person, or having many conversations and fights with this person in your head. Codependent tendencies in our relationships should be expected for men in recovery. With the emotional maturity we gain through working the Steps, we can gain a sense of autonomy and security that allows us to genuinely care for our partners as free and autonomous adults like us.

✝

MEN, VIOLENCE, AND TRAUMA

I felt less than. I was very shy,
uncomfortable, didn't want to be
the center of attention. I remember
at camp when one of the fellows hit me
in the head with a rock—stupid boy
games—and it pissed me off
and I hurt him.

– JUAN –

Juan continues:

I hit him hard and remember the fear on his face as he was lying down and me crying out loud to "fight like a man." That image of me in my mind is one of those formidable experiences. I think that something clicked there that said: "It's okay, there's a tool you can use any time if somebody hurts you or rejects you. That's your go-to option."

Do you remember when you realized that anger, or even violence, seemed to protect you from feeling hurt, rejection, fear, and other painful and unwanted emotions? Most of the men I interviewed could identify some point in their lives when they realized they were no longer allowed to express certain feelings or behaviors—especially crying.

Trying to block a punt during a fifth-grade football game, Jo ended up with the ball stuck in his helmet face mask:

I'm standing there with this ball sticking out of my forehead. I pulled the ball off and started crying. I thought everyone was looking at me and thinking I was a sissy. Two years later, I remember grabbing and tackling, and throwing this kid so hard on the ground his helmet came off—I just shattered the guy. I stood over him, and he started crying. I remember thinking, "You sissy!"

Jo has learned to act differently in recovery:

I grew up thinking that as a man you either dealt with problems physically by hitting someone or you ran away. Finally I'm learning to deal with what's going on inside of me.

You may be asking, "How is this related to the Twelve Steps?" This is a conversation that every man in recovery should have with his loved ones and his brothers in recovery to begin to explore the connections between violence and the abuse and trauma they've experienced.

Trauma

One of the most significant breakthroughs in addiction treatment is our growing understanding of trauma. Dominique talked about beginning to understand how trauma has affected his life:

I grew up with a father who was quite abusive in his discipline. I would normally expect punishment for doing anything wrong. I show all the symptoms of PTSD [post-traumatic stress disorder]. I have problems with my back, neck, and shoulders because I tend to sleep in a defensive and curled-up position.

According to the *Diagnostic and Statistical Manual of Mental Disorders,* an event is traumatic when both of the following are present: "(1) the person experienced, witnessed, or was confronted with an event or events that involved actual or threatened death or serious injury, or a threat to the physical integrity of self or others, and (2) the person's response involved intense fear, helplessness, or horror."[1] One of the distinguishing factors with trauma is not the event as much as the response to the event. It's very important to understand that if you've had a traumatic experience and still suffer from it, this does *not* mean you're weak, sick, or that you are in any way at fault.

So many men in recovery—even those in long-term recovery—are relapsing, losing marriages, disconnecting from others and their Twelve Step communities, abusing loved ones, and acting out in other ways because they are still caught up in anxiety, anger, rage, and depression as a result of untreated trauma. No matter how hard a man in this state works the Steps, the pain, confusion, and hopelessness will often remain with him. His loved ones and friends might see him as a "dry drunk" even though he has not been using alcohol or other drugs for some time.

Do you think you might be living with untreated trauma? If so, here are some questions that can help you find an answer:

- *Do you yell at other people or put them down in mean and hurtful ways?*
- *Do you find yourself mistreating your partner and sometimes feeling as if you are possessed or two different people?*
- *When you feel close to someone, do you often find yourself shutting down or becoming full of rage toward him or her?*
- *Do you mock your partner or become very uncomfortable when he or she cries or expresses vulnerability?*
- *When you feel sad or hurt, do you often turn to anger or isolate in depression?*
- *Do you overreact to conflict with extreme engagement or avoidance?*
- *Are you easily startled?*
- *Do you find yourself struggling with violent thoughts on a regular basis?*
- *Do you push others away with sarcasm, ridicule, or abuse when they are getting too close?*
- *Do you push away people you love and care about by using anger to protect yourself from being hurt?*
- *Do you have visions or fantasies of hurting those you love?*

If you answered yes to any of these questions, you should consider getting professional help if only to explore any questions you have or to get more information. Can going to meetings and working the Steps help you? Absolutely and without question. But if you're still suffering from a past trauma and expressing it in ways that may become harmful to yourself or others, you should also seek counseling.

Break the Silence

Men's abuse has been shrouded in silence for a very long time. What seems clear is that we are very confused about what is acceptable behavior toward boys and men. While we have less silence in Twelve Step communities than in our society as a whole, silence nevertheless exists, casting a long shadow over many in recovery. Only recently have we started to make a connection between the violence and abuse perpetrated on boys and men, how we are raised in this society, and the violence we commit. We need to find a way to raise boys that honors them as future men whom we want to live in emotional, physical, intellectual, and spiritual balance.

How many men have experienced abuse, be it sexual, physical, or emotional? A large number of men in treatment reported experiencing some form of abuse or neglect. A significant majority of men who were sexually abused as children do not report it until they are adults. These men often cause a significant amount of damage to themselves and others because of how deeply they buried their secrets. Much abuse is also underreported for both men and boys in part because our culture teaches boys and men that it's not okay to express pain and suffering. Conventional wisdom is that if you admit you have been abused, you then admit that you are weak because real men can handle anything! So, men suffer the abuse and then suffer with the abuse. And then, to complete the cycle, too many men in turn abuse others.

Every man I spoke with had experienced some degree of emotional or verbal abuse, while many spoke about actual physical abuse, too. Brian talked about the abuse he experienced from his mother:

> At times she was emotionally and physically abusive to me and my siblings. I remember being slapped, kicked, beaten with pots and pans, punched in the face, tackled, and belittled, sometimes for no reason. We were not to talk about these things outside of the home, despite sometimes having visible bumps and bruises.

The silence that Brian was forced to keep regarding the abuse caused a lot of pain in his teen years, and ultimately, it was a factor in his early use of alcohol and other drugs and his suicide attempts. The impact of that abuse and his efforts to heal from it lasted long into Brian's recovery.

A small percentage of men have admitted to having been sexually abused. Gary talked openly about the abuse he experienced growing up:

> My childhood abuse was quite painful. My father went to prison, and my mother was very self-absorbed. I was sexually assaulted by one of the neighborhood kids and really didn't feel safe to bring that home.

You may still believe that the abuse you grew up with was simply the discipline of your caregivers. You may talk about being hit as a child and laugh while you are talking. Or you may remember past abusive experiences matter-of-factly—as if you were reporting on the weather or last night's activities. If we listen closely, we'll hear many men telling us that they suffered abuse, even when they may not realize or believe it themselves. One of the first times men acknowledge any type of abuse is during a Step Four inventory. They may be talking about a resentment, a fear, or some part of their sex inventory, and then offer a subtle—or not so subtle— acknowledgment of past abuse. Many of us have spirits that are broken in ways that are hard for others, and even our- selves, to understand.

Walking Wounded

Boys and men tend to externalize any abuse or trauma we experience, which means we take it out on others. Stop and think for a moment—have you committed some form of abuse while in your addiction? What about during your recovery?

Mike J., a man who used to physically abuse his wife before he got sober, talked about this:

Sure, I always felt remorse, guilt, and sadness, and then I'd ask myself: "Why did I do that?" But then I'd do it again. It was just anger that I couldn't control. I had no emotional control. The only way I knew how to release emotions was through violence. My parents were that way . . . Maybe I learned it from them . . . That's just what I did.

You may be able to identify with what Mike J. is saying. You may feel ashamed of your past behavior and ashamed that you cannot talk to anyone about it. Just remember that your secrets will keep you sick. If you do not talk about your experiences with someone you trust and if you do not get help, it will be difficult for you to heal emotionally and to stay free of your addiction.

Dan J. grew up with violence in his home. Even though he hated it, he has struggled with his own anger and violence in relationships:

My wife and I had a few fights where I became so enraged I had to leave the house. Once, when she tried to stop me by taking my keys, I pushed her against a wall.

And for him, that was the wake-up call. He knew he needed to get help. And he did. He immediately called his sponsor, stayed at a friend's house, and got into counseling with a specialist in dealing with anger. He talked about the benefits of counseling both for himself and his partner. Today, Dan J. has a better understanding of the triggers for his rage and violence, and he has learned that it is okay for him to trust others with his feelings of shame, insecurity, hurt, and fear.

Brandon spoke candidly about the seemingly contradictory—some might even say insane—impulse some men have to hurt those closest to them: "There were many whom I wanted to hurt, and many whom I did hurt—namely those who were close to me—good friends and girlfriends were the ones I would target." Those urges to hurt that Brandon experienced are likely connected to the abuse he experienced when he was younger. He spoke about how the abuse he experienced as a young boy still haunts him as an adult:

I was emotionally and physically abused. It took me some time to really see the emotions I had [were] tied into my resentment of my father for the abuse. I remember when he would call us worthless, no good, and so on. Nothing was scarier than being the worthless person I feared my dad said I was. That fear has persisted.

Many men in recovery, and maybe even you, know exactly what Brandon and these other men are talking about. You may think other men wouldn't understand or don't have the same experiences, but there are those who will understand if you keep talking, even if your experiences aren't exactly the same. What's more, you may have been living with this pain for so long that you have simply come to accept it as normal—as simply your reality.

Many men in recovery still live a painful cycle of acting out, shame, and making amends. They think that this is all the Steps have to offer them. But the Steps can also help you end this cycle. As Andy said, "I was a hurt person, and I was compelled to hurt others as a result." In talking about his experience with past abuse, he told about the healing he was able to accomplish at a men's retreat. He said, "I dumped a good portion of the lies I'd been holding about my father as a result of twenty-seven years of physical, emotional, sexual and psychological abuse." Quinn, who experienced all types of abuse as a child, said:

> *Transformations slowly happen as I allow myself to love all that was not loved. The abuse happened in my youth. I have lived in a safe world since then and have tried to use it for healing.*

Rethinking Violence

When you think of violence, do you visualize assaults, shootings, or killings? Those images of violence are merely the tip of the iceberg. In the chapter on Step Four, we talked about seeing anger differently. You may now need to redefine your view of violence, too. The following are also forms of violence:

- *Raising your voice at your partner in an effort to intimidate or silence.*
- *Using your physical body to intimidate in any way by size and strength alone. Most men are intimidating to women and children, and few men understand this.*
- *Slamming doors.*
- *Threatening harm to yourself or to your partner.*
- *Punching or kicking a wall or door with someone else in the room.*
- *Taking car keys or doing anything else to prevent your partner from leaving your presence or your home, or doing any other act that prevents your partner from seeking safety.*
- *Chasing your partner as he or she tries to leave or escape from you and your threatening behavior.*

Did this list surprise you? Did you witness or experience these behaviors growing up? Have you done some of them? Have you always considered them violent? Were they on your Step Four inventory or your Step Eight list? Do you mention them to your sponsor or talk about them in meetings? If you have committed any of these behaviors in a current or previous relationship, find someone you can trust and talk about them. Then get professional help. The behavior has to stop. You have to realize that you have choices and are responsible for the choices you make.

You Are Responsible

You may have no idea why you act the way you do. You may feel that you have no control over your actions or that you are possessed. Again, this is the effect traumatic experiences can have on people.

You are not responsible for what was done to you as a child nor can you erase the traumatic events you experienced as an adult or while active in your addiction. When you have experienced abuse from others you can easily believe that you deserved it. You take on the messages of the abuse and the abuser, which tell you that you are worthless, unwanted, and unlovable. No matter how well you pretend that everything is great in recovery, the pain will still scream back at you. As Charlie put it:

> *I was punished physically in ways that shattered my trust and safety. Through much work and support I have learned to trust myself and my process.*

Do not let shame keep you silent; do not let the lies inside you control your life.

In recovery, you are entirely responsible for your life and your choices. If you aren't, who will be? You are responsible for getting help and making sure the damage stops. You are responsible for your vulnerability, fear, and softness, as well as for your anger, rage, and violence. You are responsible for healing your hurt. Nobody can do the work for you. Until you are willing to take steps to heal your pain and take full responsibility for the choices you make, you will not be free.

The Violence Is Real

We cannot ignore the very real impact that wounded men are having on this world every day. Much violence is created by men, and often it stems from our wounds. Many of us have been raised on violence. In addition to the incredible amount of violence we witness on television and other media, many of us have grown up with violence in our homes, neighborhoods, schools, and communities. Violence is embedded in men's lives.

I know that today alone, more than four thousand women will be raped or physically assaulted by an intimate partner. While both male and female children are at risk for abuse, females continue to be at risk throughout their lives while the frequency for adult males drops considerably. I know that today, some men in recovery will act violently and destructively toward women, other men, children, and themselves. I am overwhelmed writing these words.

Nevertheless, I remain hopeful and optimistic. I have seen the transformation in my own life and many other men's lives. Yes, the violence is real, but the healing and the transformation are real, too. We have to tell the whole story!

We Will Know Peace

The seeds of domestic violence and rape are planted with every young man who is abused and teased. They're planted, too, when a crying young boy is told to toughen up, when he is hit for his misbehavior, when he's made fun of for being sensitive or afraid. The seeds are many. The solution for much of the world's anger and violence depends on our evolving to a point where boys are raised to be men who are aware of their full range of feelings and are allowed to be who they are. I believe that this solution is at the heart of our evolution as a race.

Very few men are naturally violent and abusive. These extreme behaviors are the cancer of how we raise men in our society. At the heart of men's violence is self-hatred and deep disconnection from our emotional and spiritual selves. They are the result of a society that breeds self-hatred rather than self-respect and self-love. While these horrible actions are attempts to gain power, they grow out of deep feelings of powerlessness. This violence can and must end! The solution begins with each of us because we can change the world—one man at a time.

If you have any concerns about how abuse, violence, or trauma may be affecting your recovery, again I strongly encourage you to seek professional help. Do not be afraid to explore this issue; you can do it and you deserve to be truly "happy, joyous, and free"!

RESPONDING
TO DIFFERENCE

Differences ring out loud and clear
in all the outside issues. But AA works
and keeps life simple for me. I don't feel
different, black, African American or
short in AA. That's positive.

– JOE P. –

The Steps help us deal with the issues that we don't like to talk about—the ones lurking in the shadows of our recovery and the recovery community. How we all respond to, appreciate, and honor ours and others' differences can be one of the tougher challenges we face in recovery.

The tradition of "singleness of purpose"—helping the addict who is suffering—is a core tenet of the Twelve Step community. At the heart of the matter is the fact that whether someone is male, female, transgendered, gay, straight, white, black, old, Jewish, Christian, atheist, Ph.D. or high school drop-out, democrat, republican, rich, or poor simply isn't relevant. We are asked to carry the message regardless of what a man looks like, where he is from, whom he loves, or any other difference. We put his recovery from the suffering of addiction above all else.

A significant part of responding to differences depends on us developing two qualities not traditionally considered masculine—compassion and empathy—and another that's even more important: love. Joe P., who is an African American man and grew up during the civil rights era in Harlem, talked about this:

> *I learned from my experience, strength, and hope to treat people as I would like to be treated. I want to be loved and to love others. It was a journey to learn to love myself as a man and to love other women and men.*

Our Twelve Step culture sometimes has unspoken preferred values. Many meetings have a strong suggestion of Christian prejudice when the "God Steps" are discussed. Most meetings—until very recently (and even now, mostly in metropolitan areas)—unless designated otherwise, assume all attendees to be heterosexual. Much of the male gender language in the Big Book often spills over into discussions of the Steps and can subtly exclude women. For these reasons, special-interest closed meetings are prevalent now in Twelve Step communities—for gays, lesbians, and transgender individuals, people of color, Christians, women, men, and even certain professional groups. Dominique, a former priest and gay man with seventeen years sobriety, said that meetings solely for gay men were not available when he first got sober. He started attending such meetings later in his recovery. "I appreciated the opportunity it gave me to be a part of a gay recovery community," he said. Dominique continues to attend one all-gay meeting per week, but unlike some of his peers, he also believes he benefits from going to non-gay meetings, too.

The issues of other drug addiction, race, religious affiliation, class, sexual orientation, gender, and so on have been in the stories of the Big Book for decades. These stories are powerful examples of how individuals, when loved with compassion and understanding, can recover in the Twelve Step community no matter how they are different. Our common bond is far greater than any of the differences we bring into our recovery. These stories show what many of us know intuitively—the wisdom and healing power of the Twelve Steps are universal.

What's the Difference?

We interact with and have relationships with people who are different from us every single day; differences can be in gender, sexual orientation, class, education, religion, ethnicity, and skin color—to name a few.

We have emotional responses—some strong, some minor—to the people with whom we interact based on how much we see them as being similar to or different from us. We may carry judgments about the differences we perceive. We would be fooling ourselves to pretend that we are not different from one another and that we don't react to those differences and have prejudices based on them.

Larry, a white psychologist with twenty years of sobriety,

has been working hard to learn how to respond to his and other people's differences:

I want to know about someone's differences because knowing enriches and broadens my world view. This has helped me have a greater understanding and appreciation of all of the other journeys in recovery.

How much significance we apply to the differences we see is the core of this issue. How do you treat people who are different from you? How do those people treat you? Are there certain differences you can accept? Some you cannot, and if so, why not? What do the principles of the Twelve Steps tell you about how to deal with others who are different?

In the Company of Men

Often in the face of prejudice, it's easier to be accepted by our friends or a group or get some cheap laughs than to challenge each other to be the best men we can be in all our affairs. Casey, who is of Irish American descent, said:

I've witnessed homosexuals feeling very uncomfortable in some meetings and never coming back to men's meetings again. There are 60 of us, it's never addressed—some even get a chuckle out of it.

When asked why he thought this happens, he answered very honestly in a way that probably describes many of us:

I'm not willing to step up and let people know that I am uncomfortable with their behavior. I want to be part of the guys, and I don't want to be seen as weak or a momma's boy.

All men in recovery need to look at these issues if we want to grow in our recovery and deepen our emotional sobriety. Mike H., who has almost forty years in recovery and is a white CEO of a treatment center, said it this way:

I do not think men can stay sober if they do not start to look at how they treat women, people of color, or anyone who is different from them. Especially white guys, but all men. You just can't be fully successful in recovery and maintain those negative attitudes and beliefs.

People Who Would Normally Not Mix

Many of the men talked about how, as a result of their participation in recovery and Twelve Step meetings, they have met, befriended, and sponsored men whom they'd otherwise never have met or liked. As Rob said:

Being in recovery has given me the opportunity to associate with people whom I would not have otherwise known. They may be different from me in sexual orientation, race, religion, economic, and many other demographic differences, but we have recovery in common, and I see these people as peers for the first time in my life.

Many men—no matter how they were different—communicated the same theme: it might be different in the outside world, but in Twelve Step meetings, with our primary purpose, they could look beyond their own or others' differences and focus instead on the common solution of recovery. Reggie, who is African American and has twenty-one years of sobriety, said:

It would be a mistake to make too much of my being a man of color in AA. AA culture has a way of neutralizing differences. We all have the goal of sobriety and travel the same path. Our meetings have a level of connectedness that could greatly benefit society.

Gary, a gay food addict with twenty years in the Twelve Step community, said:

> *The more I act like a man who happens to be gay, rather than a gay who happens to be a man, the better off I am. The less of a big deal I make about it the better off I am.*

While it may seem simplistic or even naïve, many men seemed to be saying that what matters the most is how you respond to your difference.

I would encourage you to reflect on the following questions. There are no right or wrong answers. Instead, thinking about them will give you a chance to look at how you interact with and respond to specific differences:

1. *When attending your meetings, how does the group deal with difference? Is it simply an outside issue? How does difference show up in conversations in fellowship outside of the meetings? Are different groups made fun of, ridiculed, tolerated, or appreciated? Are they welcomed?*

2. *What do your meetings look like? Are they mostly men (and women) from the same culture? How many men of color are in your meetings?*

3. *Do you have overt use of Christian messages and beliefs at your meetings? Is there respect for the God of many understandings? Is there a place for those who are atheist or agnostic?*

4. *Does fellowship after a meeting require a certain amount of money? Is there an awareness of men's*

various economic situations when fellowship locations are decided?

5. *How many openly gay men are in your meetings? How are they treated? Do men make openly homophobic comments or jokes in the meetings or at fellowship?*

‍

EPILOGUE:
A ROOM FULL OF MEN

As men, we have a long way to go
toward integrating a sense of self
in a world that has many "false gods"
for men and women alike.

– QUINN –

Do you remember a time when somebody said: "Now you are a man"? Even if that event happened, did it really make a difference to you? Did it actually help you feel more like a man? When did you finally feel like the transformation to manhood was complete? How did you know? How do you know? Our society has lost sight of the importance of rituals to honor the changes that we all go through in passing from adolescence to adulthood. Helping a young man find his way into manhood is easier in cultures where the roles of men and women are more clearly defined. What are common rites of initiation for young men today? Having sex for the first time? Getting drunk for the first time? Going off to college and then getting drunk or having sex for the first time? Is this the best we can do? These young men are trying to find their way, and we adult men, who are supposed to help them, may still be lost ourselves. Or perhaps we're still hanging on to an idea of being a man that we do not want or know how to change. Jo talked about the generational impact of how many men are raised:

> *It's taken quite a long time for me to understand that when I want to get away, shut down, or run away, that's a part of my disease. Not just the disease of alcohol, but the disease of what it is to be a man, what it takes to be a man because that's how I learned it from my father and grandfather—you never deal with problems, you just shut down.*

We must not let history define us. Just because men in our culture have been a certain way for decades or even centuries does not mean that you and I have to be that way now or in the future. Today, who we are and how we express ourselves is changing in profound ways. Gone in modern industrialized cultures like the United States is the safety of such clearly defined roles for men and women. Gone are many of the assumptions that told us what it means to be a man or a woman. We may be on the cusp of a major social evolution in which we are seeing tremendous growth in positive portrayals of men as fathers, spouses, lovers, and friends over the past two decades. Andy, who's been in recovery and doing men's work for over two decades, commented on this change:

> *First and foremost, there are masculinities—plural. Our culture has a powerful socializing effect on what appropriate masculinity is. However, men's liberation is about redefining and expanding the range of what can be labeled* masculine, *because men*

are now doing different behaviors than ever before and gaining acceptance.

We are taking an interest in the inner, private lives of men. Pay attention to men's conversations in the media, and you hear them opening up to one another, talking more openly about feelings and their struggles in relationships. You will see portrayals of men who want to be fathers and husbands, and who show that they have emotions and consciences. I'll give you an example. A recent beer commercial depicted a guy looking for another man to watch his cat while he was out of town. After several men make fun of him for even having a cat, one man finally offered to help. Then the voice over said, "Genuine beer for a genuine man." This is a depiction of masculinity we would not have seen just ten years ago!

We all have ideas of how we are supposed to act and think as men. Most of us do not think that we can actually choose which ideas to accept. When I first started talking with men in recovery about men's issues, it resonated with them regardless of age, sexual orientation, race, creed, ethnicity, or whether newly sober or long into recovery. All seemed to want to be more than what society has offered us as men.

Some men in recovery step out of the traditional masculine roles without even realizing they've done so. We hug other men, talk about and express all of our feelings, and have intimate relationships because that is what you do when you are in recovery. Brian said:

*I have learned to survive getting my feelings hurt, being rejected
as a person, experiencing disappointment when a sponsee fails,
having my advice ignored or rejected, and so on—all critical life
experiences that encourage personal growth. My definition of
what it means to be a man has definitely broadened as a result
of working the Steps.*

Other men in recovery will die clinging tightly to some
of the masculine scripts they were given long ago, not knowing that the tools that liberated them from alcohol and other
drugs could also have liberated them from the view of masculinity that limited their personal growth and relationship
experiences.

The Limitless Possibilities of Masculinity

When we have confidence in who we are as men, we have
the ability to live our lives wearing the rest of the world and
all of its expectations of us—real and imagined—as a loose
garment. We can choose how we want to be as men in this
society. Brian talked about how he has grown and changed
as a man in recovery, "I have learned as much by viewing
what I see as undesirable characteristics of men (and rejecting them) as I have desirable characteristics (trying to emu-
late them)."

When we try to sort through how we want to live our
lives as men, it's still wise to keep sight of what is powerful
and beautiful about traditional masculinity. Joe H. said:

*While I have moved away from some of the traditional male
qualities, others are still part of me; they're not negative. Society
seems now to view most, if not all, traditional male qualities as*

bad. I do not believe they are; they are only bad if they are used in a disrespectful way.

Much of who we are is rooted in our maleness, and it will always be so. The question we have to ask is, "How do I want to express that essential part of who I am?" All of the men identified taking responsibility for your actions and being accountable—wonderful and powerful traditional masculine qualities—as essential to building a successful life in recovery. Many of our male qualities—honor, honesty, integrity, decisiveness, humility, courage, protectiveness—are lost as a result of our addictions. Fortunately, we can recover them through working the Twelve Steps.

Some of us grew up with male role models who displayed these qualities; others did not. Regardless of how you were raised, recovery gives you the opportunity to embrace those qualities. Dan J. said his idea of being a man was to be:

strong, independent, in control, run the family, the breadwinner, and help the woman by doing mechanical and construction jobs around the house. Since recovery, I have learned that these are all useful and sometimes admirable traits, but they do not define me as a man. I have also learned that it is okay to be sensitive and to cry.

One aspect of masculinity is not better than another. We are who we are. We do not need to reject the strong and silent type any more than we need to reject the family man, the communicator, or the sensitive man. We do not have to force ourselves into the false choice of one or the other.

We also cannot lose sight about what makes men different from women. First, men and women are obviously physiologically different from one another. Most men and women approach life differently—perhaps driven by the mixture of our genetics and our socialization; our nurturing and our nature. We are different, and that is wonderful.

Brandon said that most of the time when people are talking about masculinity, they are referring "to the embodiment of stereotypical masculine qualities. I am a man, so I aim to be masculine, but I also aim to be feminine or androgynous in some regards." I asked men what traditional feminine qualities, if any, they saw themselves having. Dave who has been a stay-at-home father for all three of his children said:

I am empathetic, maternal, tender, and loving. I have a love of language and conversation . . . My role as a stay-at-home dad has expanded and nurtured these feminine qualities. Some days I am a woman in that I'm in a role traditionally filled by women.

Obviously, Dave does not believe that he turns into a woman when his wife is at work, but he does understand that as his family's primary caregiver for their children, the classic female job, his "feminine" qualities have grown, and he is okay with that.

Rich, almost in a defiant tone, felt strongly that the attempt to say something was solely an attribute of men or women was limiting and did not support his experience in recovery. He said, "There is not a stereotypically positive or negative trait that would generally be associated with women that I have not seen in myself or in other men."

Now that Steve is more open about his feelings and pain, the process of recovery has also helped him see women differently. "Embracing in myself traits that are traditionally seen as feminine is not a sign of weakness; if anything, it's a sign of being more human and genuine," he said. Steve is referring to many men having grown up believing—consciously or unconsciously—that women are inferior. The last thing any guy holding that view would want is to have any feminine qualities.

All men have feminine qualities to varying degrees, and by rejecting them we reject part of who we are—and that sets us up for a deep dissatisfaction and fuels our addiction. Vang said it best:

I am masculine in that I am comfortable as a man. I am the complete human that Carl Jung wrote about as I express femininity and masculinity.

Attempting to distance themselves from the restrictions of the male stereotype and to embrace the feminine qualities they possess, many men I interviewed talked about how they wanted to see themselves more as humans than as men. Steve said, "Being in recovery has made me consider myself more human with a somewhat undefined line between masculinity and femininity." The feminine qualities Steve now sees in himself were there all along, even though he denied or rejected them out of shame and fear. In embracing those qualities, Steve is embracing his humanness.

Many men felt that living according to the Twelve Step principles of recovery was a better way to judge who they were than deciding whether they were acting like men. Rich talked about this idea when he said, "I find compassion, tolerance, and honesty to be desirable human traits, but not particularly masculine ones." Rich went on to say that his wife not only has these same qualities, but she's been the model for him as he tries to express and practice them. Brandon summarizes what I heard from many men, "I strive less to be that manly character and instead try to be a good person."

What we cannot forget is that we are men and because of that, we must be responsible for how we live in this world as men. If we only see ourselves as human, then we may not see how this world favors us—simply for being men—just as we cannot ignore how the world favors those of us who are white men or straight men. Yes, recovery offers us the freedom to live our lives being the best men we can be, but it also teaches us to do whatever we can to help others find that same freedom. When our freedom might come at the expense of another, neither of us is free and we suffer. When we understand this and use the principles of the Twelve Steps, we will listen to the voices we once ignored, we will reach out to those with whom we never sought to connect, we will come to love those we thought undeserving of our love, and we will find ourselves better understanding what it means to be "happy, joyous, and free."

Joe P. gave a wonderful example of how he is teaching his sons to be men:

I teach my sons that there are options, and they learn from me. They see what we do, every day. They see me surrounded by healthy men. They are watching us. They see that I am a healthy man. I did a rite of passage for my son when he was sixteen. I brought together men of all ethnicities and backgrounds who are in recovery, and we talked about what it was like for us at age sixteen.

What may seem a simple solution can transform a young man's life. But in the end, only you can determine what kind of man you will become.

NOTES

Feelings

1. Interestingly enough, during the 1700s and 1800s it was acceptable to express emotion, affection, and vulnerability as evidenced in correspondence from that time between men, and also between men and women. Expressing feelings was seen as normal. There is no reason we can't learn to be more expressive today.

2. *As Bill Sees It* (New York: Alcoholics Anonymous World Services, 1973), 288.

Step One

1. *Twelve Steps and Twelve Traditions,* softcover ed. (New York: Alcoholics Anonymous World Services, 1981), 21.

2. *Alcoholics Anonymous,* 4th ed. (New York: Alcoholics Anonymous World Services, 2001), 22–23.

3. God, grant me the serenity to accept the things I cannot change, the courage to change the things I can, and the wisdom to know the difference.

Step Two

1. *Alcoholics Anonymous,* 4th ed. (New York: Alcoholics Anonymous World Services, 2001), 55.

Step Three

1. *As Bill Sees It* (New York: Alcoholics Anonymous World Services, 1973), 95.

2. *Twelve Steps and Twelve Traditions,* softcover ed. (New York: Alcoholics Anonymous World Services, 1981), 40.

3. *Fresh Air* with Terry Gross, National Public Radio.

Step Four

1. *Alcoholics Anonymous,* 4th ed. (New York: Alcoholics Anonymous World Services, 2001), 64.

2. *Alcoholics Anonymous,* 4th ed. (New York: Alcoholics Anonymous World Services, 2001), 133.

3. *Alcoholics Anonymous,* 4th ed. (New York: Alcoholics Anonymous World Services, 2001), 64.

4. *Alcoholics Anonymous,* 4th ed. (New York: Alcoholics Anonymous World Services, 2001), 67.

5. *Alcoholics Anonymous,* 4th ed. (New York: Alcoholics Anonymous World Services, 2001), 67.

6. *Alcoholics Anonymous,* 4th ed. (New York: Alcoholics Anonymous World Services, 2001), 66.

7. *Alcoholics Anonymous,* 4th ed. (New York: Alcoholics Anonymous World Services, 2001), 64.

8. *Alcoholics Anonymous,* 4th ed. (New York: Alcoholics Anonymous World Services, 2001), 67.

9. *Alcoholics Anonymous,* 4th ed. (New York: Alcoholics Anonymous World Services, 2001), 68.

10. *Alcoholics Anonymous,* 4th ed. (New York: Alcoholics Anonymous World Services, 2001), 69.

11. *Alcoholics Anonymous,* 4th ed. (New York: Alcoholics Anonymous World Services, 2001), 69.

Step 5

1. *Alcoholics Anonymous,* 4th ed. (New York: Alcoholics Anonymous World Services, 2001), 72.

2. *Alcoholics Anonymous,* 4th ed. (New York: Alcoholics Anonymous World Services, 2001), 72.

Step 7

1. *Twelve Steps and Twelve Traditions,* softcover ed. (New York: Alcoholics Anonymous World Services, 1981), 72.

Step 8

1. *Twelve Steps and Twelve Traditions,* softcover ed. (New York: Alcoholics Anonymous World Services, 1981), 57.

Step 9

1. *Alcoholics Anonymous,* 4th ed. (New York: Alcoholics Anonymous World Services, 2001), 77.

Step 10

1. *Alcoholics Anonymous,* 4th ed. (New York: Alcoholics Anonymous World Services, 2001), 84.

2. *Alcoholics Anonymous,* 4th ed. (New York: Alcoholics Anonymous World Services, 2001), 67.

3. *Twelve Steps and Twelve Traditions,* softcover ed. (New York: Alcoholics Anonymous World Services, 1981), 90.

Step 11

1. Mel B., *New Wine: The Spiritual Roots of the Twelve Step Miracle* (Center City, MN: Hazelden, 1991), 12–13.

2. *Alcoholics Anonymous,* 4th ed. (New York: Alcoholics Anonymous World Services, 2001), 87–88.

3. *Twelve Steps and Twelve Traditions,* softcover ed. (New York: Alcoholics Anonymous World Services, 1981), 103.

4. Carlos Rodriguez is cited as the author on the Web site www.poemhunter.com.

Step 12

1. *Alcoholics Anonymous,* 4th ed. (New York: Alcoholics Anonymous World Services, 2001), 89.

2. *Alcoholics Anonymous,* 4th ed. (New York: Alcoholics Anonymous World Services, 2001), 77.

3. Center for Substance Abuse Treatment, *The Epidemiology of Co-Occurring Substance Use and Mental Disorders,* COCE Overview Paper 8, DHHS Publication No. (SMA) 07-4308 (Rockville, MD: Substance Abuse and Mental Health Services Administration and Center for Mental Health Services, 2007), 1.

4. *Alcoholics Anonymous,* 4th ed. (New York: Alcoholics Anonymous World Services, 2001), 133.

5. *Alcoholics Anonymous,* 4th ed. (New York: Alcoholics Anonymous World Services, 2001), 164.

6. *Alcoholics Anonymous,* 4th ed. (New York: Alcoholics Anonymous World Services, 2001), 89.

Men and Relationships

1. This section is about men caring deeply for each other whether they are gay or straight.

2. Melody Beattie, *Codependent No More* (Center City, MN: Hazelden, 1986), 36.

Men, Violence, and Trauma

1. *Diagnostic and Statistical Manual of Mental Disorders,* 4th ed., text revision (Washington, DC: American Psychiatric Association, 2000).

Dan Griffin, M.A., has worked in the mental health and addictions fields for over two decades. Griffin is the author of groundbreaking resources for professionals working with men: *A Man's Way through the 12 Steps, A Man's Way through Relationships: Learning to Love and Be Loved,* and coauthor of *Helping Men Recover* with Stephanie Covington, Ph.D., and Rick Dauer. Griffin travels internationally, educating and training clinicians and other professionals about how to effectively work with, intervene on, and treat men. In early 2010, he started a consulting, training, and speaking business, Griffin Recovery Enterprises. He served as the state drug court coordinator for the Minnesota Drug Court Initiative from 2002 to 2010, and was also the judicial branch's expert on addiction and recovery. His masters research was on the social construction of masculinity in the culture of Alcoholics Anonymous, the first qualitative study of its kind. He has worked in a variety of areas in the addictions field: research, case management, public advocacy, drug courts, adjunct college faculty, and counseling. He is a highly sought after speaker and trainer who has presented to thousands of people from around the world. Griffin is a proud husband and father and has been in long-term recovery since graduating from college in 1994.

Hazelden, a national nonprofit organization founded in 1949, helps people reclaim their lives from the disease of addiction. Built on decades of knowledge and experience, Hazelden offers a comprehensive approach to addiction that addresses the full range of patient, family, and professional needs, including treatment and continuing care for youth and adults, research, higher learning, public education and advocacy, and publishing.

A life of recovery is lived "one day at a time." Hazelden publications, both educational and inspirational, support and strengthen lifelong recovery. In 1954, Hazelden published *Twenty-Four Hours a Day*, the first daily meditation book for recovering alcoholics, and Hazelden continues to publish works to inspire and guide individuals in treatment and recovery, and their loved ones. Professionals who work to prevent and treat addiction also turn to Hazelden for evidence-based curricula, informational materials, and videos for use in schools, treatment programs, and correctional programs.

Through published works, Hazelden extends the reach of hope, encouragement, help, and support to individuals, families, and communities affected by addiction and related issues.

For questions about Hazelden publications, please call **800-328-9000** or visit us online at **hazelden.org/bookstore**.